## Alone at the Plate

He pulls on the helmet, picks up the bat,
 and walks to the plate, "gotta hit and that's that."

The crowd starts to yell, the game's on the line,
 last inning, two outs, the score's nine to nine.

Dad yells, "Go get it," Mom wrings her hands,
 coach hollers, "hit it" but alone there he stands.

Heros are made in seconds such as this,
 but he's just a little boy, what if he should miss?

Years after this game's ended and he's little no more,
 will he remember the outcome or even the score?

No he'll have forgotten if he was out, hit, or a run,
 he'll only look back on his friend's and the fun.

So cheer this boy on, alone with his fate;
 help him remember with fondness, this stand at the plate.

Spend your time wisely and help in his quest
 to be a hitter with confidence and always his best.

And when the game's over, this boy can stand tall,
 for you've helped him prepare to give it his all!

# You Can Teach
# HITTING

**DUSTY BAKER**

**JEFF MERCER**

**MARV BITTINGER**

**B²**

**BITTINGER BOOKS, INC.**

Carmel, Indiana

*A Subsidiary of Howard W. Sams & Co.*

Published by

Bittinger Books
3011 Whispering Trail
Carmel, IN 46033

and

Masters Press (a subsidiary of Howard W. Sams)
2647 Waterfront Pkwy E. Dr., Suite 300,
Indianapolis, IN 46214

The photograph of Dusty Baker on the cover and page v and the photograph of Will Clark on page 14 are reproduced courtesy of the San Francisco Giants and Martha Jane Stanton.

Not all of the drills and exercises contained in this book are suitable for everyone and the use of this or any program could result in injury. Readers should consult with a qualified professional to determine which of these exercises are suitable for a specific individual.

Responsibility for any adverse effect or unforeseen consequence resulting from information contained in this book is expressly disclaimed.

**Library of Congress Cataloging-in-Publication Data**

Baker, Dusty, 1949–
        You can teach hitting / by Dusty Baker, Jeff Mercer, and Marv
    Bittinger.
            p.        cm.
        Includes index.
        ISBN 0-940279-73-8
        1. Batting (Baseball)    I. Mercer, Jeff, 1960–        . II. Bittinger,
    Marvin L.    III. Title.
    GV869.B29 1993
    796.357'26—dc20                                                        92-1119
                                                                            CIP

# Introduction

## The Book

What kind of book can you expect from an outstanding major-league player and batting coach of 24 years, a highly regarded hitting instructor and coach of 12 years, and a university mathematics professor and best-selling textbook author?

Well, *You Can Teach Hitting* is a serious book about fun. After all, it's about baseball, and anyone who's watched or played baseball knows that's fun. And it's about hitting a baseball, and anyone who's hit a baseball knows what fun that is, even if they don't hit it well—or even frequently.

But most of all, *You Can Teach Hitting* is about *teaching hitters a systematic approach to hitting a baseball*—better and more consistently. And for good coaches, teaching young people how to get more fun out of their game is a serious matter at any level.

Unlike other books, *You Can Teach Hitting* provides an adaptable, step-by-step approach to hitting that will help anyone—from the encouraging parent to the experienced coach—teach the fundamentals of hitting to players of all ages, at all levels. And if you're a hitter, it's an excellent source for self-evaluation and improvement.

Although you'll find the book crammed with tips for advanced hitters, hitting drills, and situational hitting exercises, *You Can Teach Hitting* is about fundamentals. And like the great hitters, it returns to the fundamentals again and again.

Like a good textbook, it presents a clear and systematic approach to fundamental hitting skills that can be taught—and learned—by anyone who opens the book. It looks at the ten most common mistakes hitters make and how you can help your players eliminate them, systematically. And it provides lots of optional batting exercises consistent with your hitters' individual needs *within* the overall approach.

The techniques described in the book are easier to visualize because we have used a multitude of four-color photographs and figures to illustrate them. We think these features make our approach in *You Can Teach Hitting* exceptionally clear and easy to teach.

We have also produced a *You Can Teach Hitting* companion video series for this volume. Information on purchasing the videos can be found at the end of the book.

## *The Collaboration*

It should surprise no one that baseball—a game of numbers, percentages, averages, and symmetries—holds numerous attractions for a professor of mathematics. But it's my unvarnished love for the game that led me to the baseball fantasy camps, where I met Dusty Baker, and to the instructional facility, where I met Jeff Mercer, my eventual collaborators on *You Can Teach Hitting*.

*San Francisco Giants/Martha Jane Stanton*

**Dusty Baker as hitting coach for the San Francisco Giants.**

What struck me immediately about Dusty—and stuck with me throughout the writing of this book—is his teaching method and manner. His warmth, patience, and good humor and generosity make him a great teacher and, doubtless, they've played their part in developing hitters like Will Clark, Kevin Mitchell, and Matt Williams—each of whom won National League RBI titles during Dusty's first three years as the Giants' batting coach.

**Dusty as a player for the Los Angeles Dodgers hitting a three-run homer in the third game of the 1977 World Series.**

AP/Wide World Photos

Dusty, of course, brings to coaching and *You Can Teach Hitting* some rather impressive hitting credentials of his own, beginning with a .321 batting average in 1972—his first full season with the Braves—12 points off Billy Williams' league-leading .333. In 1981, with the world champion Dodgers, Dusty's .320 average was the third best in the league.

In league championship play, he posted a .371 average and .579 slugging percentage through four championship series. And if you were a Phillies fan in 1977, you'll remember Dusty's .357 average and incredible .857 slugging percentage (including two game-winning home runs, one a grand slam), leading the Dodgers to the National League pennant and earning himself the series' first MVP award.

During 19 major league seasons, Dusty compiled a .278 lifetime batting average, hitting better than .300 four times and flirting with that magic number four other times. He stroked 242 home runs, drove in 1013 runs, and collected 1981 hits (only 19 shy of the 2000-hit plateau reached by only 147 major leaguers). A complete ballplayer, Dusty won both Silver Slugger and Golden Glove awards during his career.

But it's Dusty's ability to work with and bring out the best in hitters of all skill levels—including my fantasy camp teammates and young people in his baseball school—that make his contribution to *You Can Teach Hitting* so invaluable.

My other collaborator, Jeff Mercer, and I met at his Mercer Sports Complex in Indianapolis, where I was preparing myself for another baseball fantasy camp. For better than 12 years, Jeff has coached baseball at virtually every level of play, from Little League to Indiana University to the Indiana Amateur Baseball Association—all with equal success. Along the way, he's produced All-State scholastic players, scouted big league talent for the Mets, and yearned to produce a book on hitting.

In 1989, Jeff's approach to hitting lifted Indiana University's team batting average from .303 to .353, first in the Big Ten and second in the nation. That Hoosier team set eight offensive records and produced Indiana's first Big Ten batting champion since 1976, Bill Jordan. This year, Mike Smith, another of Jeff's Indiana University recruits, won college baseball's Triple Crown.

Eight of Jeff's hitters have moved on to the professional ranks, most notably, Mickey Morandini of the Phillies and John Wehner of the Pirates.

It's no wonder Jeff's the most highly respected hitting instructor in Indiana. His hitting philosophy and teaching style have proven flexible enough to develop hundreds of hitters of all ages at all levels. And his rare teaching ability, along with his experience and knowledge of the game, has gone into *You Can Teach Hitting*, making it unique among instructional hitting books.

As for me, I'm a full-time baseball fan and part-time coach. Incidentally, I'm also a full professor of mathematics education at Indiana University–Purdue University at Indianapolis, where I've authored more than 110 textbooks, selling over six million copies.

In collaborating with Dusty and Jeff, I've been able to bring to their thoughts on hitting my experience as a teacher, a writer, a learner, and a coach. As a teacher, I've contributed some insight into their approaches to teaching hitting that have resulted, I hope, in making those approaches more explicit and accessible to the reader.

As a writer, I've brought some hard-won knowledge about what makes a book of instruction actually work for the reader—and what makes it an effective teaching and learning tool.

As a player and coach, I've brought a teaching conviction of mine—shared by Dusty and Jeff and assumed throughout the book—that, generally speaking, disciplined hitters are best developed with patient coaching. And most important, along with patience and dedication, coaches need to care.

MARV BITTINGER
1993

# About the Authors

**Johnnie B. "Dusty" Baker**, an outstanding hitter through fifteen major league seasons, is the batting coach for the San Francisco Giants, where he's helped develop hitters the likes of Will Clark, Matt Williams, Robby Thompson, and Kevin Mitchell. Dusty is also the co-owner of the *Dusty Baker School of Baseball* for ages 8 to 20 in Sacramento, California. In 1990, Dusty was inducted into the United States Black Hall of Fame and the Sacramento Sports Hall of Fame.

**Jeff Mercer** teaches baseball at his Mercer Sports Complex in Indianapolis. The most highly regarded hitting instructor in Indiana, Jeff is a former assistant coach at Indiana University. Jeff brings a knowledge and experience of the game that will improve you as a coach or hitter.

**Marv Bittinger**, teacher and author of better than 110 mathematics textbooks, selling over six million copies, contributes his writing talents and unrestrained love of the game to this unique collaboration.

We hope the book is beneficial in leading the coach to being a better hitting coach, the player to being a better hitter, and the parents to being successful teaching their children. We want to hear from you regarding your opinions of the book and how it affected your baseball life. Please write to us in care of:

BITTINGER BOOKS
3011 Whispering Trail
Carmel, IN  46033
(317) 846-9136

Good luck and great hits!

Dusty, Jeff, and Marv

# Acknowledgments

The authors wish to acknowledge those who assisted in the preparation of this book.

For many helpful comments and "pinch hits," Emmett Carney, Jerry Hester, Mark Langill, Ron Marinucci, Bill Poole, Jim Strapulos, Russ Umphenour, Dave Wiley, and Larry and Valerie Bittinger.

For "gold glove" editing and "grand slam" book design and layout, Martha Morong and Geri Davis, at Quadrata, Inc., of Wakefield, Massachusetts. For "clutch" editorial assistance, copy editing, typing, and rewrites, Judy Beecher, Doe Coover, Tom Dwyer, Cyrisse Jaffee, and Patsy Hammond.

And for "coming off the bench" to provide creative, prompt, courteous printing service, Lois Halcomb, Julianne Young, and Mark Burke at PIP Printing in Indianapolis.

Because this book teaches through visualization, we would be remiss in not applauding the exceptional artwork, photography, four-color, computer-enhanced graphics, and composition "laid down" by Tech-Graphics in Woburn, Massachusetts. "High fives" all around to Jim Sullivan and his team, including Rosa Bancarotta, Steve DeFuria, Eugene McDonough, and Greg Urbaniak.

And a special tip of the cap to Jim Sullivan for his masterful direction of the *You Can Teach Hitting* video series. Its quality owes much to Jim's creativity, hard work, and dedication.

Our hitters—Harold Campbell, Tim Hester, Kyle Lonzo, Angie Rapp, Andrew Sylvester, Nick Sylvester, Mark Wiley, Rosa Bancarotta, Emmett Carney, and Eugene McDonough—all deserve a standing ovation for standing in at the plate through long photo and video sessions—and not taking an intentional walk.

Special "applause" also goes to Steve Walsmith for his inspiring lithography and poem "Alone at the Plate," which appears at the beginning of the book.

These major leaguers offered advice with many technical issues in the last chapter, and we thank them wholeheartedly:

Carl Erskine, former pitcher for the Brooklyn and Los Angeles Dodgers;

Clem Labine, former pitcher for the Brooklyn and Los Angeles Dodgers;

Reggie Smith, former player for the Boston Red Sox, St. Louis Cardinals, and Los Angeles Dodgers, and now minor league hitting coordinator for the Dodgers;

David Wallace, minor league pitching coordinator for the Los Angeles Dodgers.

And a special thanks to Hall-of-Famers Hank Aaron and Billy Williams. Hank Aaron reviewed and endorsed the final version of the manuscript. Billy Williams graciously penned its Foreword.

## Some Personal Acknowledgments

We each want to take a minute or two to thank some people who have touched our lives variously and profoundly.

***Dusty Baker:*** "When you play and coach in the major leagues as long as I have, many people affect your hitting and coaching philosophy. In a sense, we are each a product of those who have touched our lives. Thanks to all those who helped me develop as a professional player and coach. In particular, I would like to thank Hank Aaron, Tommy Davis, Roy Campanella, Joe Black, Ralph Garr, Billy

Williams, Pete Rose, Joe Morgan, Willie Mays, Willie Stargell, Al Oliver, Eddie Mathews, Spider Jorgenson, Bill Lucas, Bob Lucas, Jim Gilliam, Dick Allen, Bob Veale, Sandy Koufax, Bobby Bonds, Tony Perez, Al Campanis, Clete Boyer, Reggie Jackson, Joe Rudi, Joe Pepitone, Reggie Smith, Ray Hale, Clyde King, Mickey Vernon, Curt Flood, and Gary Matthews.

I'd also like to acknowledge those who influenced me early in life, including my American Legion coach, Spider Jorgenson; my junior high coach, Rudy Morales; and my high school basketball coach, Eli McCullough. Most of all I'd like to thank my supporter, believer, and mother, Christine Baker, and my own Little League coach—and coach in real life as well—my father, Johnnie B. Baker, Sr."

*Jeff Mercer:* "Thanks to Bob Morgan, head baseball coach at Indiana University, for his guidance and knowledge of the game.

I would also like to give special thanks to my parents, Roger and Joan Mercer, for giving me the chance to play the game and for all their encouragement. A special thanks is owed my wonderful wife Pam for her unwavering confidence and support. Thanks also to my boys, Jeff, Dan, and Joe, who never cease to inspire me."

*Marv Bittinger:* "First, I thank Bart Kaufman, my close friend whose persistence got me to that first baseball fantasy camp where I met Dusty.

I would also like to thank my two fine sons, Lowell and Chris, who have been my pals through life. Together we have played and attended so many sporting events, as well as enjoying other adventures such as hiking and traveling. My heartfelt thanks also goes to my wife and best friend, Elaine. Words cannot adequately express my thanks for her constant support of my writing, and her patience in enduring all my sporting and coaching ventures while raising me as her third 'son.' "

# Foreword

The need for informed instruction in baseball hitting ranging from youth through high school, college, and the minor leagues is tremendous. A book that begins at a fundamental level and builds carefully on those concepts would be invaluable. I feel that Dusty Baker is eminently qualified to be involved in such an instructional book.

Among today's major league baseball players, a camaraderie has been lost. When Dusty and I played major league baseball 5 to 20 years ago, there weren't too many days that we didn't go to the ballpark early and stand around the batting cage talking about hitting not only with our own teammates but even with the opposition. Later, when the League banned such fraternization, we lost on two counts: the friendships we made and the valuable information we shared about hitting. Since we were both from Mobile, Alabama, Henry Aaron of the Atlanta Braves and I would often get together. Others with whom we became good friends were Dusty Baker and Ralph Garr, also with the Braves. When the Cubs were in Atlanta, the four of us might have barbecues and talk hitting. Or we might gather in the clubhouse for an hour or two after the game. When Atlanta was in Chicago, Dusty, Hank, and Ralph would come to the Cubs' clubhouse. Each of us became better ballplayers through this interchange and friendship.

The 1972 season was a challenging season since the three of us—Ralph and Dusty with the Atlanta Braves and me with the Chicago Cubs—were involved in the batting race. It was exciting for me because earlier in my career many people predicted that my smooth swing, which they compared to that of Ted Williams, would land me a batting title someday. Toward the end of the season I was

*June, 1964; Billy Williams was hitting .400 as a Chicago Cub.*

AP/ Wide World Photos

concerned because both Dusty and Ralph were hitting the ball real well. Each of us wanted that batting title! After playing during the day at Wrigley Field, I would try to pick up the Atlanta Braves' game in the evening on the radio if they were playing in, say, Cincinnati or St. Louis. The intense competition that season only heightened my respect for both Dusty Baker and Ralph Garr. I finally won the batting title with a .333 average, but Ralph Garr was a close second at .325 and Dusty third at .321.

In baseball today, there is too great an emphasis on winning and losing rather than learning the fundamentals. Players simply don't know enough about hitting. A book like this, which provides a base for young hitters that can be extended to high school baseball, then college, and on into the pros, will help to fill a void that currently exists in the instruction of younger players.

In my own experience coaching in the minor leagues, I saw a large gap between the hitting abilities of minor leaguers and those of major leaguers. I would hear surprising questions like "Do I step in the bucket?" or "Do I step into the ball?" I was so stunned by their lack of ability that I found myself asking the scouts or the farm director, "Who signed these guys?" By returning to teach at the minor league level, I did realize that those players are trying to learn and are in great need of proper instruction.

Dusty Baker is an outstanding hitting coach for many reasons, not the least of which is that he worked very hard to move from the minors up to the majors. Being a hard worker in the minor leagues is not only batting practice, however. Dusty has spent years reading many books and magazines and studying countless films and videos. Some players who were excellent major league hitters are just not able to relay their skills to other players. Dusty is different. He has the knack of teaching hitting. He can get into the head, mind, and body of a hitter to

*Billy Williams played major league baseball with the Chicago Cubs from 1959 to 1974 and with the Oakland Athletics from 1975 to 1976. In 1970, his most productive year, he led the league in runs scored (137) and hits (205). In 1972, he won the batting title with a .333 batting average. He was elected to the Hall of Fame in 1987 and now serves in the front office with the Cubs.*

Wide World Photos

instruct him on not only the fundamentals but also all the special details, both physical and mental, that make a hitter successful.

Dusty also excels at teaching the mental part of hitting. Every baseball player gets into periodic slumps. Much of a player's hitting depends on his mental attitude on a particular day. If you don't think you can hit a pitcher, the odds are that you won't. You must have a positive attitude every time you step up to the plate. One of Dusty's greatest assets was his positive attitude. Even if he went 0–4, he'd always say, "I'm going to get 4 or 5 hits tomorrow." He knows how to impart this self-confidence to those he teaches as well.

Dusty also knows that caring about your players only helps you to communicate your expertise to them. The San Francisco Giants have a good hitting ball club because of Dusty Baker. The players see his caring personality and react positively to it. Dusty's been through the baseball hitting wars. He knows about the mental and physical game and enjoys working with his players. One of the most satisfying things you can hear as a hitting instructor is a player saying, "I see what you're saying."

There are many baseball books out on the market. But one directed toward the young player and his parents is different. Teaching a youngster the fundamentals is one of the most important things we can do in baseball today. He will never lose that valuable information, but will build on it as he moves through the youth leagues into high school and college.

BILLY WILLIAMS

# Contents

*Introduction*    vii

**About the Authors**    xi

**Acknowledgments**    xiii

*Foreword*    xvii

**1    A Teaching Philosophy for Parents, Coaches, and Players**    2

**2    Hitting Fundamentals**    14

**3    The Ten Most Common Hitting Mistakes
and How to Correct Them**    46

**4    Hitting Drills**    72

**5    Offensive Weapons**    104

**6    Practice Organization for Teams**    118

**7    Approaches to Hitter Development**    130

**8    The Hitter's Mind**    158

**9    The Advanced Hitter**    176

*Appendix*    **Where Do You Go From Here?**    223

*Index*    232

You Can Teach

# HITTING

# CHAPTER ONE

# A Teaching Philosophy for Parents, Coaches, and Players

Our Teaching Philosophy

The Characteristics of a Good Coach

Motivating Your Players

Improving Hitting Skills

**Marv.**  *Many coaches affected your career. Can you tell us about some of your amateur coaches and describe their assets?*

**Dusty.**  The first was my dad, Johnnie B. Baker, Sr. He was my Little League coach. He cut me from the team three times for having a bad attitude. Although I was upset at the time, I understand now. My dad got me on the right track as far as attitude is concerned. He taught me what it takes to be a professional and conduct myself like a man.

Another was Spider Jorgenson, my American Legion coach. His assets were not only his overall knowledge of the game, but also the fact that he was an amateur coach who was an ex-professional. He told me what to expect when I got into professional baseball. He was very, very patient and possessed an even demeanor.

Another who had an even temperament was Eli McCullough, who was actually my high school basketball coach. Both games are related as far as thinking is concerned. He was very caring and a big help to me when I had family problems. He taught me mental toughness and how to think. He also taught me to have high dreams and goals.

M ost players agree that hitting is the most enjoyable part of the game of baseball. At the same time, however, it is the hardest skill and one about which many people know the least. This book provides step-by-step information on hitting instruction that can be helpful to both parents and coaches who work with children age 4 and older. Its unique approach also enables motivated players to teach themselves to become better hitters.

Throughout this book we use the word "coach" to mean "baseball teacher," that is, anyone who is helping to teach the game of baseball. Parents, coaches in the usual sense, and players themselves can all be baseball teachers. Although most of the hitting philosophy in this book applies to softball as well, its main direction is baseball.

We also use the pronoun "he." Although many girls play baseball, most players, especially age 15 and older, are boys. Therefore, the use of "he" seemed most practical and convenient, but is not meant to discriminate.

# Our Teaching Philosophy

Our teaching philosophy has developed as the result of the many hours we have spent working with players at all age levels. We believe that the goal of any coach is to get the most out of *all* players and to make sure that each player has progressed to *his* satisfaction and ability level.

Of course, baseball is only a game and is meant to be fun, but at the same time it's important to define what "fun" means in this competitive sport. For most players and coaches, *true* fun in baseball lies in working hard, improving one's game, and playing with others as a well-coordinated team. Having a winless season isn't fun. Trying to convince your team otherwise is not being honest with yourself or your players. Working hard toward the goal of improving one's skills, and then achieving that goal whether the team wins every game or not, is not only enormously satisfying, but makes the "work" of team practice seem like "play."

Sometimes "fun" is confused with "no effort." It's often a challenge to ensure that players have fun and work hard at the same time. But in order to truly enjoy the game and have the opportunity to improve, players need direction and discipline, including a schedule of well-run, organized practices. Without these, players won't be able to focus and concentrate on their goals and play well. When players are motivated to devote their time and energy in organized practice, they will be able to perform well both individually and as a team.

**Our teaching philosophy is:**

- To have *fun*;

- To establish a proper learning environment, in which *improvement* is the goal;

- To convey a *positive, upbeat* attitude;

- To be *patient* and *caring* with players;

- To make efficient use of time by having *organized* practices and games.

## The Characteristics of a Good Coach

The key to training and motivating players is a good coach. Oddly enough, knowing every aspect of the game is not as important as knowing how to communicate with players. A coach who is not particularly knowledgeable can nevertheless have a dramatic effect on his players by conveying a sense of dedication, commitment, and love for the game. Although they may not acquire many new skills or techniques, the players of such a coach will work hard, enjoy the game, and feel that they have gained a lot. By the same token, an authority on the game who cannot communicate well with his players won't create the kind of environment that is conducive to learning or improvement or fun. Indeed, we have seen instances time and time again in which such coaches have driven players out of the game.

An old saying goes, "You can catch a lot more flies with honey than you can with vinegar." Of course, people respond to praise much more readily than to criticism. It is important in baseball—as it is in life—to be upbeat and positive. Whenever a coach must say something negative to a player or a team, it's extremely helpful if he uses a considerate tone or ends on a positive note.

A coach should be patient with the needs and problems of his players. It can help to be aware of the players' other interests and talents, such as academics, hobbies, musical trends, or popular television shows. Sometimes a related comment about a non-baseball topic will do a lot to make the players feel that you care about them and their concerns.

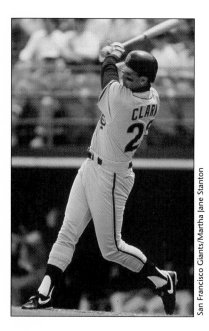

San Francisco Giants/Martha Jane Stanton

"This game is a lot of fun. If you don't have fun, you're not going to succeed. So, you've got to let the kid go out there and fail a little bit in order to succeed, and at the same time, he's got to have some fun. He can't have pressure on him all the time to win, win, win. I've seen a lot of kids dislike the game and shy away from it because they're pressured too much. Pressure sometimes turns to rejection."

Will Clark, San Francisco Giants

So many of the baseball "lessons" that a coach will teach his team are also significant lessons in life: It's important to respect one's fellow players and competing teams, make good grades in school, be responsible, plan ahead, and achieve goals by hard work. If a dedicated player needs extra time to study for an important test, excusing him from a scheduled practice will show that you recognize the value of the player's schoolwork. Such a time conflict also provides an opportunity to discuss an important lesson for all players: To be part of a sports team, one must carefully budget one's time.

A good coach lets his players know that he cares for them as individuals rather than just as a means of winning a baseball game. Make an effort to set time aside to talk one on one with each team member to become better acquainted and to discuss his abilities and goals—not just in baseball but in everyday life. Be sure, however, to offer your attention evenly so as not to create jealousy or rivalry.

No matter what type of coach you happen to be—positive or negative, quiet or vocal—it is worth your time to consider periodically the attitude

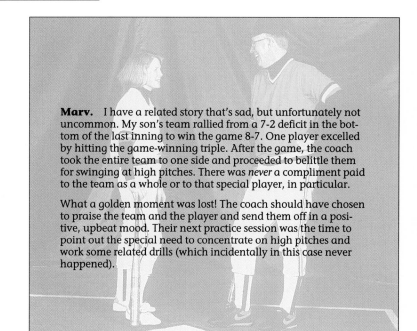

**Marv.** I have a related story that's sad, but unfortunately not uncommon. My son's team rallied from a 7-2 deficit in the bottom of the last inning to win the game 8-7. One player excelled by hitting the game-winning triple. After the game, the coach took the entire team to one side and proceeded to belittle them for swinging at high pitches. There was *never* a compliment paid to the team as a whole or to that special player, in particular.

What a golden moment was lost! The coach should have chosen to praise the team and the player and send them off in a positive, upbeat mood. Their next practice session was the time to point out the special need to concentrate on high pitches and work some related drills (which incidentally in this case never happened).

that you present to the players. Whether you are a volunteer or a paid instructor, it is important that you examine and evaluate your style of coaching. Is your approach working? Is it having a positive or a negative effect on the team as a whole and on individual players? Do you show displeasure with your team's performance in a constructive manner, or do you react by stomping your feet, turning your back, and rolling your eyes?

If your team is having problems, don't automatically blame your players. Maybe you need to work harder with them. For example, let's say that your hitters are struggling with curveballs. Do you respond simply with anger, or do you devote extra practice time to strengthening the skill of hitting curveballs? Whether your team is practicing or playing, make sure that you work as strenuously as they do and put forth all possible effort in improving their game.

## Motivating Your Players

For players to function well, a coach must maintain a disciplined and organized environment. Keep in mind, though, that a group of nine- or ten-year-old players is not able to perform with the agility or maturity of a college baseball team. They do not have the attention span, physical ability, or sense of direction of a group of 20-year-olds. Raising your voice constantly will not always ensure cooperation. You must earn the respect of your players, as well as establish your authority with them. To that end, it is important to establish these two rules immediately:

1. Players must keep their eyes on the coach when he is talking, paying close attention to all that's said.

2. Players should put forth every possible effort during the time they are with the coach and the team.

Baseball relies on mental toughness because a player endures such a mental game within himself. If a player gets caught up in that mental game, however, it becomes a detriment to his performance.

Baseball is the only team sport in which a player depends so much on himself while so many other people are depending on him as well. When he hits, he is up there alone. His team can help him only with moral support. The battle is the hitter against the pitcher. It is as simple and as complicated as that, and yet the result of his at bat may determine whether the team wins or loses. That's a big burden to place on a young person!

---

**"KEEP IN MIND THAT A GROUP OF NINE- OR TEN-YEAR-OLD PLAYERS IS NOT ABLE TO PERFORM WITH THE AGILITY OR MATURITY OF A COLLEGE BASEBALL TEAM."**

Almost every young ballplayer really *wants* to be the best that he can be, even if he doesn't have the physical ability he'd like. It is important to capitalize on this desire. Unfortunately, by the age of 11 or 12, many players drop out of competitive baseball, often because it is too difficult for children at this age to handle failure. Part of their inability to cope with failure, however, may lie more with the inadequate or inappropriate behavior of the coach. If a player is not successful at bat, particularly in a critical situation, it is often too easy for the coach to come down hard or give up on him.

Although it's *never* appropriate to be abusive or insulting, if a player makes a physical mistake due to a mental mistake (he didn't concentrate or got lazy mentally), you should not hesitate to give him direct and explicit feedback. Make sure he understands what went wrong. Most players know that when they make a mistake due to a lack of focus, they deserve some constructive criticism. Players resent being criticized, however, when they feel that, despite their failure, they have honestly put forth their best effort.

Young people appreciate consistency. If they know that they can count on you to be encouraging instead of enraged and helpful instead of belittling, they will be willing to listen to your comments. If you can correct them by explaining exactly what went wrong and teaching them how to avoid repeating their mistake, they will be better able to accept the criticism and will want to work hard to improve. The

## For The Advanced Hitter.........................................

*"For major league hitters, I carry out the same strategy as above. For some hitters, I say something immediately. For others, I have to wait until they cool down. Such a move is always a touchy one. Some coaches think you should wait until after the game. But what happens to the outcome of the game, if the hitter is allowed to make the same mistake for three more at bats? For major league hitters, it is especially helpful to let them be natural until something correctional is needed."*

Dusty Baker

coach who helps to salvage something positive out of one failure at bat may ensure that the next at bat is successful.

If you need to criticize a hitter, choose the moment very carefully. For some players, immediately correcting an error may do more harm than good because they are already hard enough on themselves. Approaching such a player after the game might be more effective. Other players may be more receptive to instant feedback and not particularly concerned if you correct them on the spot. This is an example of how important it is that you get to know your players individually. What

works for one will not always work for another.

Let's say that the hitter strikes out on a pitch in the dirt. Should you allow him to let that affect the next two at bats and possibly strike out again? Or could your immediate input, whether criticism or advice, help the player to hit a double off the right centerfield fence? It is important that you be able to make that decision quickly in most cases. Keep in mind, however, that hitters can consistently "bounce back" from failure only if they know that the person they admire and respect most on the team—their coach—is consistently behind them.

If a hitter truly believes that he can hit and visualizes himself being successful, that confidence will virtually guarantee that he will succeed, regardless of his level. "Potential" will take a player nowhere if he does not have character, pride, and heart. You can take a .300 average high school hitter

> "The most successful coach is not one who gets the most out of his top players, and not even one who gets the most out of the good players. A truly outstanding coach is one who can take the below-average hitter and elevate him to a higher level."

and make him a .400 hitter if he has the will to achieve that goal. It's better to have a team full of lions with heart, drive, and desire, than a team full of potentials with absolutely no heart, no drive, and no desire.

It's easy for a hitter to make the mistake of dwelling on his past performance and letting it dominate his future actions. A hitter cannot change the past. The only thing he can control is what he does next. The fact that he struck out earlier on a called third strike must have no bearing on his next trip to the plate.

Since for many high school or youth league teams, a season may consist of only twenty games, a five-game slump is critical. It means that one fourth of the year is lost! Therefore, a hitter cannot afford to be down five games of the season. He must try to bounce back immediately with every at bat. If he has no hits after the first two at bats, he must tell himself that he *will* get a hit the next time up. If he gets a hit, then he tries for two hits. The coach's refrain should be: *Always remember that if you do not do well today, come back swinging tomorrow!*

Too many players pack it in and quit when they have a bad day. The successful hitter never gives up. He struggles to do better and better, withstands failure, and returns the next day working even harder. With a good bit of guidance and instruction and a lot of support from his coach, a good hitter will be able to demand the best from himself.

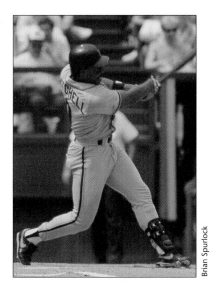

Brian Spurlock

A good coach never allows a player to believe that success is impossible. If you hear a player say "I can't," immediately tell him, "Yes, you can. You are just not doing it right now. You're not succeeding yet, but you will." If the player knows that your approach is helping him become a good hitter or even a great hitter, he'll believe you and welcome your firm encouragement. The most successful coach is not one who gets the most out of his top players, and not even one who gets the most out of the good players.

A truly outstanding coach is one who can take the below-average hitter and elevate him to a higher level. Often a team becomes the league champ not because the superior players performed to their ability, but because the weak players with whom the coach has patiently worked come through with winning hits.

## Improving Hitting Skills

Have you ever visualized how tough it is to hit a baseball? The hitter is swinging at a round object (the ball) with an oblong, round object (the bat). It is very difficult to make contact in order to make a hit. A very slight angle change can mean the difference between a ground ball, a line drive, or a pop-up. It takes 0.44 of a second for a 90-mph fastball to reach the plate from a pitcher's hand. *That's less than half a second*—a very short time for a hitter, under pressure, to make a decision about whether to swing at a pitch and then to hit it correctly.

How can coaches actually help their players to become better hitters, both physically and mentally? The first task is to emphasize, on a daily basis,

"About hitting – do not ever get upset with yourself! You just thank God that there is always another day. I have a lot of players come to me asking why I do not get upset about failure at the plate. I tell them that I thank God that I am able to be here in the major leagues and that I know that I have three more at bats that day. I cannot let the pitcher know that I am upset. I tell myself that the pitcher is not getting me out. I am getting myself out."

Kevin Mitchell, Seattle Mariners

proper technique and fundamentals to help the players improve their basic hitting skills. The second task is to know the players individually. The better you know them, the easier it is to decide when to criticize and when to back off.

The third stage in making players better hitters is to provide them with the environment, direction, and format for success. You must have a systematic approach along with a blueprint for providing success, especially for a younger hitter.

The fourth stage is to encourage hitters to always be aggressive at the plate. It is a great temptation to coaches of younger players to force a player to take pitches and draw a walk, either because he is a weak hitter or because the young pitcher has a difficult time throwing strikes. This is the time, however, when the development of the player should take priority over the desire to win a game.

The coach should prefer that a hitter swing at good pitches, but he should first and foremost want that player to improve his hitting skills. Think about it! Hitting a baseball is the most difficult task in sports. If you expect a weak hitter to stand at the plate and take pitches, you have, in effect, taken the bat out of the batter's hands. The greatest joy of that player's season might be the one time he connects with a pitch. It is more important for the hitter's development that he be aggressive and swing at bad pitches than stand at the plate and not take advantage of the opportunity to learn to hit.

We also recommend that coaches do not make a practice of telling their hitters to take the first pitch. If the pitch is good, swing! Often the result of taking the first pitch puts the hitter behind in the count. Such an action gives the pitcher even more of an advantage.

Some people think that hitting is a skill that can be improved just by swinging the bat. This is not necessarily true. A hitter needs the practical knowledge that only an experienced guide can provide. The goal of *You Can Teach Hitting* is to detail that blueprint for success for the baseball teacher, whether parent, coach, or the hitter himself.

# Our Teaching Philosophy and Tips to Make Players Better Hitters

## Our Teaching Philosophy Is:

- To have *fun*;
- To establish a proper learning environment, in which *improvement* is the goal;
- To convey a *positive*, *upbeat* attitude;
- To be *patient* and *caring* with players;
- To make efficient use of time by having *organized* practices and games.

## Tips to Make Players Better Hitters

1. Emphasize proper technique and fundamentals on a daily basis.
2. Know your players individually—know when to criticize and when to back off.
3. Provide the proper environment, direction, format, and plan for success.
4. Encourage hitters to be aggressive at the plate.

# CHAPTER TWO

# Hitting Fundamentals

A Systematic Approach to Hitting

1. Bat Selection

2. Depth and Distance at the Plate

3. Stance and Balance

4. Grip on the Bat

5. Box and Bat Angle

6. Inward Turn

7. Stride

8. Swing

Conclusion

**Marv**. *What hitting trends do you see in present-day baseball players?*

**Dusty**. I see more and more players trying to hit the ball out of the ballpark. Young hitters fall into the trap of going for power before having an adequate grasp of the fundamentals of hitting.

**Marv**. *What would you say to a young hitter who seems obsessed with hitting home runs?*

**Dusty**. Power will come to some, but all hitters will be better for applying the fundamentals. What we want to promote is *good hitting*. Let the power follow naturally.

**Marv**. *Can you tell us, briefly, what you should strive for to be a great hitter?*

**Dusty**. The great hitter develops what we call the *Three C's of Hitting*: Confidence, Concentration, and Consistency. Will Clark is an excellent example of such a hitter.

In its entire history, only 7000 men have played major league baseball. Some have developed into solid, effective hitters through strength and sheer athletic ability more than through their grasp of fundamentals. Since most players, however, do not possess the physical attributes of those athletes, the average hitter can't expect to get by on ability alone. He has to learn and develop hitting skills from a sound fundamental base. Far from proposing a strategy that attempts to make clones of all hitters, we intend to provide a sound fundamental hitting philosophy that players can use to guide their individual progress. Hitters gain two advantages from such a base. One, they can use it to continually improve their hitting skills. Two, they can *always* go back to this base when struggling.

"A hitter has to learn and develop hitting skills from a sound fundamental base. Our goal is to provide a sound fundamental hitting philosophy that players can use to guide their individual progress. Hitters gain two advantages from such a base. One, they can use it to continually improve their hitting skills. Two, they can *always* go back to this base when struggling."

# A Systematic Approach to Hitting

A systematic approach to hitting becomes a framework for everything that you, as a coach*, will teach about hitting. Although this framework allows for individual variances or adjustments, keep in mind that it's very difficult—in fact, almost impossible—to be an effective hitting coach if you allow your players to hit exactly as *they* want to hit. If the players do not begin with the same hitting base, it is difficult to determine each player's progress and assess any level of improvement. In fact, such a lack of teaching structure lowers the odds of a player advancing to a higher level. In this chapter, we outline a **systematic approach to hitting** in detail.

Although many of the terms we use to explain concepts may seem childish or simplistic to the advanced coach or hitter, they have been effective teaching aids in hundreds of coaching situations through many years of experience. Young hitters will remember and use such phrases as "squish the bug" as long as they play the game!

*Recall that the term coach refers to a parent, a coach, or a hitter teaching himself.

## A Systematic Approach to Hitting

1. Bat selection
2. Depth and distance at the plate
3. Stance and balance
4. Grip on the bat
5. Box and bat angle
6. Inward turn
7. Stride
8. Swing
   a) *Focus the eyes*: Start on the eyes of the pitcher, and then move to the area of the ball at the release point.
   b) *Squish the bug*: Pivot the back foot and thrust the hips.
   c) *Slap the hands down*: Swing the bat in a slightly downward plane, through the ball.
   d) *Ike to Mike*: Keep the head down.
   e) *Follow-through*: Finish the swing.

Hitting is probably the most over-coached yet undertaught skill in all of sports. Many coaches believe that they know how to hit merely because they are older and have played the

**FIGURE 1**

**A. Bat parallel:**
**An appropriate bat.**

**B. Bat drops or quivers:**
**An inappropriate bat.**

game at some level. We do not mean, of course, to be critical of anyone who volunteers his or her time—baseball needs all the caring, dedicated coaches it can find. But hitters need a foundation, a philosophy—yes, even a plan of attack—with which to go to the plate. Once a young person understands that there are certain actions in the process of hitting that *absolutely* must go right, successful hitting becomes more achievable.

We believe that 75% of hitting is from the neck up. If a hitter truly believes that he can hit, he will hit. If he has any doubt, and most hitters do at some time, that's when he will not do well. Anyone who has ever played will probably agree with this. Good hitting occurs when there is a total focus on the pitcher, the ball, and the act of hitting. A player must learn to tune out any extraneous sights and sounds—yelling in the stands, comments of other ballplayers, movements on the field, and so on. Otherwise, he loses his concentration on what should be done at the plate and poor hitting is generally the result.

When teaching young people to hit, it is critical that you convey to them *pre-cisely* the actions that you want them to carry out when they go to the plate. There should be no gray areas. Make the tasks as simple as you can and then adjust for each player's individual abilities and differences. This is the goal of our eight-step systematic approach to hitting.

## 1. Bat Selection

The first step, proper **bat selection**, is important and often overlooked. Many young hitters, influenced by peer pressure, think about bat size more than how to use the bat effectively. And often a young hitter, particularly one between the ages of 8–12, is judged by the size of the bat rather than how well he really performs with that bat. It is better, however, for a hitter to average .400 with a light 29-inch bat than average .150 with a heavy 33-inch bat. It is one of the first responsibilities of a coach of young players to assist them with proper bat selection.

Make sure that the hitter uses a bat he can handle. A hitter has the proper bat when he can both start and stop that bat effectively (see Figure 1). Have the hitter take the bat in his stronger, or dominant hand. For most people the dominant hand is the one they use the most, but such dominance varies from person to person. If the hitter is a right-handed hitter and he also throws right-handed, then the right hand is probably the dominant hand. For the left-handed hitter and thrower, the left hand is probably dominant. Otherwise, the bottom hand (the one closest to the small end of the bat, the knob) is probably dominant. So far as the swing goes, we prefer the bottom hand to be dominant.

To determine whether the bat is appropriate, have the hitter grip the bat, in his dominant hand, all the way down at the end and hold it straight out from his body parallel to the ground—not in front, but to the side. He should try to keep his arm completely straight. If he can hold the bat for 25–35 seconds without dropping the barrel or noticing a quivering of the arm, then it is probably a bat that he can handle. If the barrel drops or it is obvious that the hitter is straining after 10 seconds, then the bat is too big and a shorter or lighter bat should be used.

The thickness of the bat handle is determined merely by whatever is most comfortable for the player.

Metal bats have become quite expensive. One way to save money is to buy a bat that is at most 1 inch longer than what might be appropriate at the time, so that it will last for two years. Until he grows into it, the hitter can use the longer bat by "choking up" —that is, moving his hands up the handle, say, 1/2 to 2 inches. Choking up, in fact, may assist in the hitter's ability to handle the bat and hit effectively.

## 2. Depth and Distance at the Plate

The second step of the systematic approach to hitting is **depth and distance**. Should the hitter stand far away from the plate, close to it, or somewhere in between? Since the pitcher already has a built-in advantage because he knows where he is throwing the ball, the hitter should not give him any further advantage by incorrect positioning at the plate. Standing too close to the plate can make a young hitter susceptible to an inside pitch, although most hitters tend to prefer such a pitch. On the other hand, a young hitter who stands too far away may be susceptible to an outside pitch.

Often, due to poor groundskeeping, there is a 3- to 4-inch hole in the batter's box where previous hitters have "dug in." Inevitably, all the hitters end up standing in that hole regardless of their height. Such a tactic makes no sense, however. The hitter should be lined up at the plate on the basis of his size, the length of his arms

"Standing too close to the plate can make a young hitter susceptible to an inside pitch, although most hitters tend to prefer such a pitch. A young hitter who stands too far away may be susceptible to an outside pitch."

# For The Advanced Hitter..................

Most young hitters, because of fear of the ball, tend to "bail out" of the box. Setting depth and distance in the preceding manner lessens this tendency and leaves the player better prepared to hit a curveball.

The advanced hitter may not follow this guideline. When finding depth and distance, he needs to take arm and leg length more into account. In the batter's box, with knees slightly bent, he places his bottom hand on the bat and extends the bat to the opposite side of the plate, just touching the edge, as shown in the figure.

Many advanced hitters set themselves too deep in the box. This renders them more susceptible to sinkers and breaking balls, because their position in the box gives such a pitch another 6 inches or so to break.

**Finding depth and distance for the advanced hitter.
A and B: The correct method.
C and D: An incorrect method.**

**A. With knees slightly bent, place bottom hand on bat and extend to opposite side of plate.**

**B. With knees slightly bent, place bottom hand on bat and extend to opposite side of plate.**

**C. Incorrect: Knees are not bent.**

**D. Incorrect: Knees are not bent.**

YOU CAN TEACH HITTING

**FIGURE 2**
*Finding depth and distance.*

Align bat parallel to line along front of plate.

Knob of bat shows where to place front foot.

Locate bat in middle of plate.

and legs, and the size of his bat, not where the hitter before him dug in.

It is important that the hitter be comfortable at the plate; thus he should, to a certain extent, be able to decide for himself where to stand. To help him do so, have the player take the bat and lay it down on the ground with the end of the bat right in the middle of the plate and parallel to the line along the front of the plate (see Figure 2). He can find the middle of the plate by noting where it comes to a point in the back. Wherever the knob of the bat ends is where the hitter places his front toe. (The **front foot** is the foot closest to the pitcher. The **back foot** is the foot closest to the catcher.)

This visual method of finding **depth and distance**—that is, the proper **depth** in the batter's box and the proper **distance** from the plate—positions young hitters properly with respect to the plate and provides them with the best opportunity to hit an inside pitch. It will also help the hitter handle outside pitches once the other

fundamentals have been properly executed.

### 3. Stance and Balance

Next the hitter needs to be in a proper **balanced stance**. Young hitters should set up a little bit pigeon-toed, with both feet turned in just slightly and spread about shoulder width apart (see Figure 3a). The purpose of the hitter being pigeon-toed is to lead to **balance.** The player's weight should be on the balls of his feet. You can test his balance by giving the hitter a shove in the chest (see Figure 3b).

**Set up pigeon-toed with feet in and weight on balls of feet.**

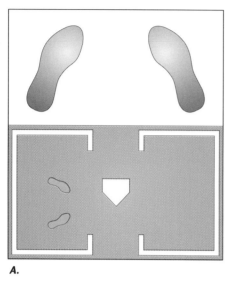

Hitter is balanced if he can resist push from coach.

**FIGURE 3**
*Determining stance and balance.*

**A.**

**B.**

If you can knock him off balance, which will normally happen the first time, he will get a better feel for where he should position the balls of the feet so that he can't be pushed over (see Figure 3c). If the hitter leans too far forward, then shove him from behind. What he needs is a well-balanced, workable stance.

The hitter can also achieve proper balance by setting himself up with his feet pigeon-toed and knees slightly bent to the point at which he would be comfortable sitting on the back of a

Hitter is not balanced if he falls back from a push from coach.

**C.**

chair or on his bat. Another trick is to have him close his eyes and find a balanced position. Usually the hitter will waver and then settle in the balanced position that is appropriate for swinging a bat.

Some major league hitters, such as Giants outfielder Willie McGee, are naturally pigeon-toed. Still others exaggerate this stance by positioning themselves in an almost knock-kneed stance, which also creates balance. Examples of such players are Pedro Guerrero, who is naturally knock-kneed, and former major leaguer Reggie Smith, who purposely placed himself in a knock-kneed stance.

A properly balanced stance translates into speed, quickness, and strength, and is very important for the transfer of weight in the upcoming swing. It is similar to the proper defensive posture of a basketball player who must move rapidly right or left to cut off a drive to the basket. It also parallels the stance of a tennis player who is prepared to return a serve. To hit effectively, the batter must be in a position to move rapidly, but stay balanced. That 0.4 second from pitcher's mound to home plate is not much time to react.

## For The Advanced Hitter.....................

The more advanced hitter need not be locked into a parallel stance. He can start either open or closed, so long as he strides toward the pitcher and ends up parallel.

*Reggie Smith in a pigeon-toed, knock-kneed stance.*

Wide World Photos

San Francisco Giants/Martha Jane Stanton

Once a workable stance has been established, the young hitter should set up in that position parallel to a straight line from the pitcher's mound to home plate (see Figure 4). The **_parallel stance_** is preferred to an **_open stance_** or a **_closed stance_**. Since the pitcher already has an advantage of knowing what and where he is going to throw, the hitter should not add to

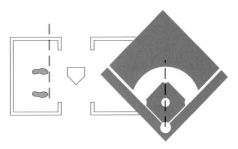

**A. Recommended parallel stance.**

"This game is about comfort. If you are not comfortable in the batter's box, you are not going to have success. If you don't have a bat that is comfortable, you are not going to have success. Don't try to stand up and copy Will Clark. Take what you have and work with it."

Matt Williams, San Francisco Giants

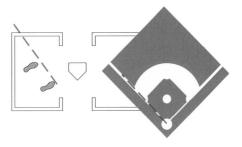

**B. Open stance.**

this advantage by setting up in either an open or a closed stance. Such positions often help the pitcher decide where to pitch. From a pitcher with some skill, a hitter with an open stance will get more outside pitches, while one with a closed stance will get more inside pitches. Thus the parallel stance is the best choice for the young hitter.

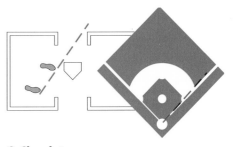

**C. Closed stance.**

**FIGURE 4**

YOU CAN TEACH HITTING

## 4. Grip on the Bat

The next stage involves the hands and the alignment of the grip—a critical point in the systematic approach to hitting. There are three different types of grip: the *standard*, the *modified*, and the *choke*.

With the **standard grip**, which we prefer for the young hitter, the player aligns the middle knuckles on both hands (see Figure 5a). A simple tip for setting up this grip is to lay the bat down in the fingers, not in the palms, across the calluses in the hands (see Figure 5b). The standard grip is somewhat similar to a golf grip, but without the thumbs on the bat. If the hitter lays the bat down in his fingers as though he were gripping a golf club and then picks it up, he will normally find that the middle knuckles on both hands are aligned.

The goal of the standard grip is to achieve with the hands and bat as much quickness and speed as possible. Think of "quickness" as how the bat starts. Think of "speed" as how fast it moves through the strike zone. An important equation from the field of physics can be applied to hitting a baseball. It says that "the distance a

## For The Advanced Hitter..........................................

*Finding a standard grip on a bat is similar to gripping a golf club. Be careful, however, that this does not lead you to think that swinging a golf club will enhance your baseball hitting. The swing of a baseball bat is not necessarily compatible with the swing of a golf club, even though the grips may be compatible. In fact, some major league managers have not allowed their players to play golf for this reason. Consult your hitting coach.*

**A. The standard grip.**

**FIGURE 5**

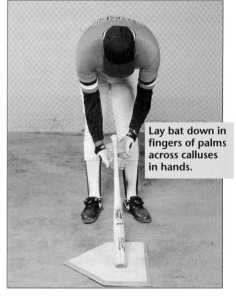

Lay bat down in fingers of palms across calluses in hands.

**B. Positioning the standard grip.**

# For The Advanced Hitter.................................................................

The advanced hitter can further modify any of the three bat grips to help direct a hit to a certain part of the field. The wrist of the bottom hand can be adjusted on the bat to send the ball to the opposite field, to center field, or to the pull field. These adjustments are shown for a right-handed batter in the accompanying photographs.

To coincide with the right-field grip, while in your stance, bring the bat closer to your body in order to create a greater push in your swing inside the ball. Using the left-field grip, take your hands away from your body. This will allow you to hit the outer half of the ball, which will help to pull it to left field.

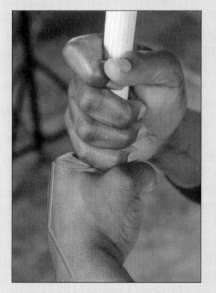

**A. Right-field grip.**

**B. Center-field grip.**

**C. Left-field grip.**

and muscling. Holding the bat in the fingers creates a looseness and whip in the swing that allows the ball to be hit crisp and hard. Take a hammer, some nails, and a thick board to practice. Have a hitter try to drive a nail while holding the hammer tightly in his palm. Then have him hold the hammer loosely in his fingers (not so loose as to let go!) and throw the head of the hammer at the nail. He will soon discover that the latter technique is more effective. The same idea works with holding the bat.

The standard grip is recommended for most hitters in order to help them maintain a more level arc on the swing through the strike zone. It also enables the hitter to **throw the head of the bat at the ball**. To do this, he accelerates his wrists, forearms, hands, and fingers and throws the bat through the strike zone. Suggest to the hitter that he think of cracking a whip rather than swinging the bat.

If you have an exceptional hitter (say, age 16, 6 feet, 3 inches, 215 pounds) who can hit the ball consistently over 300 feet, doesn't run particularly well, and will hit fourth or fifth in the line-up, you might consider moving him to a choke grip to help him get a little more lift on the ball. This will capitalize on his ability to drive in runs. However, remember that it is much more important to teach your players how to hit correctly; let the power evolve with time. Too many young hitters try to become power hitters *before* they learn to hit properly. You may have only one or two hitters out of 100, at the age of 16, who will qualify to move to the choke grip.

**"Throw the head of the bat at the ball. To do this, the hitter accelerates his wrists, forearms, hands, and fingers and throws the bat through the strike zone. He should think of this as though he were cracking a whip."**

## 5. Box and Bat Angle

The next aspect of the systematic approach to hitting is to position the hands and arms to allow the hitter to use his most effective stroke. This is

A proper box.

FIGURE 7          *A. A proper box.*

called forming the proper ***box and bat angle***. The hitter forms a box with his hands, arms, and shoulders (see Figure 7). The bottom of the box runs along the bottom forearm. The front side of the box runs up the front arm. The top of the box runs in a direct line through the shoulders, right to left, or left to right, depending on whether the hitter is right- or left-handed. The back side of the box runs down the back arm.

*"An improper box is formed if the back elbow is up. Youth league coaches commonly make the mistake of telling hitters to keep the back elbow up."*

An improper box is formed if the back elbow is up. Unfortunately, youth league coaches commonly make the mistake of telling hitters to keep the back elbow up. This is generally a misguided attempt to get the player to the point where he achieves a slight downward stroke that results in line drives and ground balls. Although this is an appropriate goal, it should not be achieved by raising the elbow.

*B. An improper box: hands too high.*

*C. An improper box: hands too low.*

A proper box: elbows feel even.

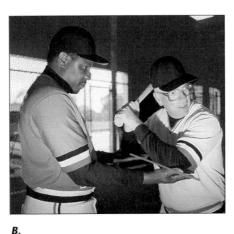

An improper box: back elbow too high; elbows feel uneven.

*A.*

*B.*

**FIGURE 8**     *Finding a proper box.*

Telling your hitters to raise the back elbow further compounds a common problem. Whenever the back elbow starts up, it must come down *before* the ball is hit. The swing then tends to get underneath the ball, which causes the player to pop up or miss the ball altogether. Whenever the hitter has an uppercut in his swing, the bat *does not stay in the strike zone very long*! Thus in order to form a proper box, the hitter must have the back elbow *down* with the upper part of the top hand about level with the top of the back shoulder. The hands should be 6–10 inches from the body. The arms should not be held out away from the body. Don't stretch the box and don't squeeze it!

To determine whether a hitter has assumed a proper box, place your hands under his elbows (see Figure 8). If the hitter has a proper box, as in Figure 8(a), his elbows will feel even. The hitter will also probably feel more comfortable than he would with his elbows uneven (Figure 8b).

Ask your players to think of their favorite hitter. It might be Jose Canseco, Ryne Sandburg, Eddie Murray, or Will Clark. Or it might be a great hitter who has retired, like Carl Yastrzemski, Rod Carew, or Hank Aaron. Regardless of who he is, everyone begins the actual swing in the same place—that is, with the top hand about level with the shoulder and with the arms form-

"In order to form a proper box, have the back elbow *down* with the upper part of the top hand about level with the top of the back shoulder."

**FIGURE 9**

The suggested
45-degree angle.

*A. Suggested: 45-degree bat angle.*

Not recommended:
a 90-degree angle.

*B. Not recommended: 90-degree bat angle.*

ing a proper box—just before coming forward in his stroke. Hitting well means eliminating as many mistakes as possible. One way to do so is to start with a good stance, and then form a proper box.

In addition to a proper box, it is also advantageous to determine the most appropriate bat angle. The angle is in a plane perpendicular to the shoulder (see Figure 9a). It is suggested that this angle be 45 degrees, with the batter laying the bat back just slightly over the back shoulder. This will allow the most natural position for the hitter. The hitter should not have the bat straight up and down in a 90-degree angle (as in Figure 9b) primarily because, like a choke grip, this will cause a loop in the swing.

## 6. Inward Turn

When a hitter has learned to set himself up in a fundamentally sound stance, the next step is to teach him to gather strength and to recognize and time pitches. Timing pitches is not nearly as critical a factor for a 10-year-old ballplayer as it is for a 17-year-old hitter, who will see variance in the speeds of pitches at the higher level of play. By the time he's older, however, the 10-year-old hitter who learned to time pitches will not be frustrated trying to hit curveballs.

Once a hitter moves to a level where the pitcher starts throwing breaking balls, it is absolutely *imperative* that he be able to recognize and time pitches. Thus it is recommended that *all* hitters learn an **inward turn**. The hitter must go backward with his weight slightly before he goes forward.

To illustrate the need for the inward turn, tell one of your young hitters that he has one punch with which to defend himself against a big muscle-bound guy. Ask him how he will go about it. You can predict that the first thing he'll do is cock back his arm. Stop him right there and ask why he did that before he swung. The typical response is, "to get a little extra power or strength." Your answer should then be, "Then why don't hitters do that?" Where does a hitter gather strength? Most hitters move from a dead stop forward—in other words, the first movement with the hands is forward. This eliminates two things, however: most of the hitter's potential for strength or speed or quickness and al-

## For The Advanced Hitter.........................................

> To take an inward turn, the advanced hitter might not go through all the preceding motions. He might tuck just the shoulder, the hip, the knee, the hands, or some combination of all four. In addition, because of strength and quickness, the advanced hitter may be able to delay his inward turn closer to the time when the pitcher releases the ball.

most any possibility of timing the pitch.

To teach an inward turn, first tell the hitter that when the pitcher shows him his hip pocket, he should do the same. That is, when the pitcher gets to his balance point and shows his hip pocket, the hitter shows his hip pocket to the pitcher. The inward turn is carried out by the young hitter tucking his front knee, front hip, and front shoulder. As a result, the hitter rolls his hands back, approximately 3 inches, but *never* behind the head. The inward turn thus gives the hitter the

strength, speed, and quickness to take a good stroke and, at the same time, provides the opportunity to time the pitch (see Figure 10).

Another advantage to the inward turn is that it lets the hitter keep his front shoulder closed until the last possible instant. He is thus able to maximize the strength, speed, and consistency of his swing by not letting the front shoulder "fly out" (open too soon). The hitter coils back to get ready to uncoil forward, out, and through the ball.

Hands back about 3 inches

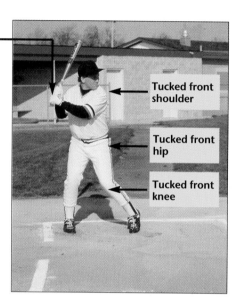

Tucked front shoulder

Tucked front hip

Tucked front knee

Hands back about 3 inches

When pitcher shows you his hip pocket, show him yours.

Tucked front shoulder

Tucked front hip

Tucked front knee

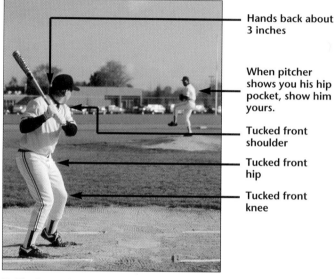

**FIGURE 10**

*A. The inward turn from the side.*

*B. The inward turn from the rear.*

## 7. Stride

Once the hitter achieves his inward turn, he is ready to take his **stride**. A common question from coaches is, How do you talk about stride? Do you want to talk about striding away or, as so many people call it, "bailing out" or "stepping into the bucket"? Do you step toward the pitcher, or do you step toward home plate? What follows is especially applicable to young hitters.

To take a stride, the hitter moves his front foot toward the pitcher as though he were actually walking away from his hands. The stride is taught in a three-step sequence, using memory devices that young players especially understand. The hitter should:

**1.** take his stride at a 45-degree angle toward home plate,

**2.** land on the big toe of the front foot, and

**3.** pretend that he is stepping on thin ice.

YOU CAN TEACH HITTING

If he lands on the outside of the front foot, he will "break the ice" (see Figure 11). The stride should be fairly short, no more than 4–8 inches, and toward home plate at a 45-degree angle. A long stride is not desirable for two reasons. First, it dissipates the hitter's strength. Second, it tends to make the bat pass underneath the line of the ball from where the batter saw it as it left the pitcher's hand. This leads to either pop-ups or swinging strikes.

The 45-degree angle is important first, to prevent bailing out and second, to keep the hitter in proper balance for any breaking or offspeed pitches. Once the hitter takes a correct stride, he is in a strong hitting position. His body weight is balanced right through the middle of his body. He is not leaning forward and not leaning back. His hands are kept back, set to react when his eyes identify a pitch different from the usual fastball. The longer the stride, the greater the tendency to bring the hands forward, which makes it very difficult to hit anything offspeed or hard and up in the strike zone.

One final tip is in order regarding the stride. Slow feet enhance fast hands, which is what the hitter wants. Quick

Foot position before striding

A. Foot position before the stride.

Foot beginning stride

B. Foot position at the end of the stride.

FIGURE 11

## For The Advanced Hitter.................................

At the end of the stride, the advanced hitter should strive to have his body parallel to a line from the pitcher through the plate. Many major league hitters begin with an open or closed stance, but finish almost parallel. For example, Jose Canseco starts open and finishes parallel, whereas Will Clark starts closed and finishes parallel.

**FIGURE 12**

A. To focus his eyes, the batter starts on the eyes of the pitcher.

B. Then he moves his eyes to the area of the ball at the release point.

feet get the hitter off balance and slow the hands, which the hitter does not want. At the completion of a correct stride, the hitter is ready to begin the swing, or stroke, the fun part—taking a good cut at the ball.

### 8. Swing

*a) Focus the eyes.* *Start on the eyes of the pitcher, and then move to the area of the ball at the release point* (see Figure 12). The hitter normally takes a few practice swings before striding. After he has brought the bat back the last time at about the instant the pitcher begins his windup, the hitter should have his head square to the ground with both eyes level and focused on either the pitcher's eyes or the bill of his cap. This gives the hitter a focal point from which he can quickly change his focus to the ball at its release point and begin identifying the movement of the pitch.

*b) Squish the bug. Pivot the back foot and thrust the hips.* The swing begins, surprisingly enough, from the waist down. There the hitter has the best opportunity to attain a lot of quickness and an excellent bat angle. At the end of the stride, the hitter has

Thrust hips

Front heel down

Pivot back foot

Thrust hips

Front heel down

Pivot back foot

*A. Squishing the bug correctly: side view.*

*B. Squishing the bug correctly: rear view.*

**FIGURE 13**

*C. Squishing the bug incorrectly.*

landed on the big toe of his front foot, pretending that he is stepping on thin ice.

Then the heel of his front foot touches the ground with the weight of the front foot evenly distributed. This is the official start of the swing. The hips are released and the swing begins (see Figure 13). The hitter next begins movement of the back foot by rolling up onto the ball of the foot and thrusting his hips. The back hip rotates toward the ball as if to hit it. The front hip rotates accordingly, so that eventually the front waist is turned to-

ward the pitcher. These first parts of the stroke are referred to simply as **squishing the bug**. The hitter imagines a bug under the ball of his back foot and squishes it by rolling that foot up onto its ball with the heel in the air.

> **"THE HITTER MUST USE HIS HIPS!**
>
> **THE HIPS LEAD THE WAY**
>
> **TOWARD THE BALL."**

When the hitter squishes the bug, he thrusts his hips into the swing as he rotates his waist and back foot. The hitter must use his hips! The hips lead the way toward the ball. Initially, they cock in the inward turn and then uncock toward the ball. The hips should not move up and out. Lack of rotation with the back foot (not squishing the bug) will prevent the hips from having any significant effect on the swing of the bat. Tell your young hitters to watch for the back foot rotation of the major leaguers. Is their swing a good

one? Part of the answer comes from deciding whether the hitter squished the bug.

*c) Slap the hands down. Swing the bat in a slightly downward plane.* The next movement is to swing the bat in a slightly downward plane through the entire strike zone. This helps the player hit line drives and ground balls.

This movement can be taught using two slapping motions with the hands (see Figure 14). Have a player stand opposite you, with his hands together out in front. His hands will simulate the ball, while your hands will simulate the flight of the bat. Hit the hands of the player with your front hand. Your other hand shows the flight of the bat and hits the others in a downward plane. If the bat (your hands) uppercuts the ball, the player's hands will move upward—not a proper swing. If his hands move downward or straight, the swing is correct. A good drill is to reverse roles, with the player slapping your hands.

Slapping the hands down is actually shown in the swing by the bottom hand and the knob of the bat first moving toward and inside the ball.

*A. Slapping the hands down: a desirable cut at the ball.*

*B. Slapping the hands up: an undesirable uppercut at the ball.*

**FIGURE 14**

**d) Ike to Mike**. *Keep the head down.* The third stage of the swing is described by naming the hitter's front shoulder *Ike* and his back shoulder *Mike*. The head of the hitter, as he looks at the pitcher, starts on Ike. When he completes his swing, it ends on Mike. Actually, "Ike to Mike" says that the hitter's head doesn't move. It stays right down on the ball. Keeping the head down is critical to helping the hitter look at the ball and get a good feel for its position and movement (see Figure 15).

**FIGURE 15**

Ike: chin starting on front shoulder

Mike: chin ending on back shoulder

*A. Ike.*

*B. Mike.*

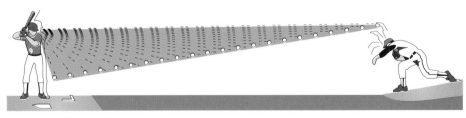

*C. Keeping the head down.*

YOU CAN TEACH HITTING

The following demonstration illustrates the value to the hitter of keeping his head down beyond the benefit of seeing the ball and getting a good feel for its position and movement. Hold your hands out as shown in Figure 16. Then tell your player to put his hands on top of yours, hold his head up, and push down as you push up. Repeat the demonstration, but this time have him hold his head down. Most hitters will notice that they are *stronger* when they keep their head down. This extra strength will be applied to the ball, because keeping the head down causes the activation of more muscles and a firmer swing on contact.

*e) Follow-through.* The final part of the swing involves getting a good **follow-through**. Many hitters stop the swing short—they make contact with the ball and then back off without completing the swing. The goal of the hitter at the point of impact should be to accelerate his hands as much as possible and drive through the ball. In other words, the follow-through is carried out by "catching" the ball with the bat as though it were a spoon and throwing the ball to the outfield. A complete follow-through is the final

Less strength in resistance with head up

**A.**

More strength in resistance with head down

**B.**

**FIGURE 16**
*Keeping the head down gives the hitter more strength.*

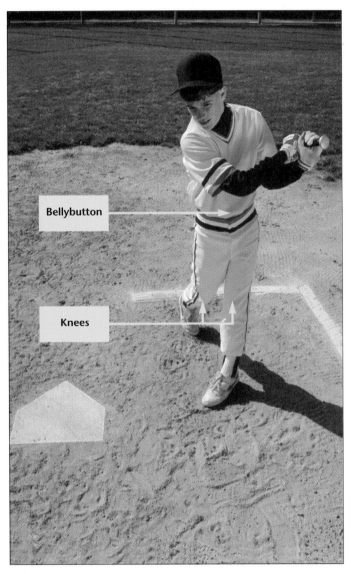

Bellybutton

Knees

**FIGURE 17**
*The "three eyes" are facing the pitcher upon completion of the swing.*

step in achieving the maximum speed on the batted ball. Remember, too, that the harder the ball is hit, the less time the players have to field it and throw the runner out.

Upon completion of the follow-through, make a final check of the swing. This ensures proper use of the hips and consists of what we call the "three eyes"—that is, both knees and the bellybutton. All three "eyes" should face the pitcher upon completion of the swing (see Figure 17).

## Conclusion

If you can communicate the specific fundamentals of this systematic approach to hitting to your players, you have made their learning much easier. It is essential that hitters memorize the steps of the approach. They should be able to recite from memory exactly what you have taught. Although some young players may not be able to execute all the fundamentals, they will know at least what steps they should be doing. By the time these hitters reach the age of 12 or 13, these skills will have become, through repetition, second nature to execute.

YOU CAN TEACH HITTING

As we mentioned earlier, hitting is the most difficult skill in all of sports. The skill will not be acquired to any degree of success unless the coach has emphasized and reemphasized the proper techniques and fundamentals. All the information in the world isn't of any value unless it's used properly. The fundamentals cannot be mentioned the first week of practice and then put aside—they must be *stressed* on a *daily* basis. Before even beginning batting practice, an instructor needs to go through the fundamental techniques of hitting whether it's the first day of practice or the hundredth. You never know when on any given day something you say will click with one of your hitters and put him over the top. Don't worry that you may sound like a broken record—the payoff will come when you see hitters using all this information to their advantage. The more you coach, the more you will refine, extrapolate from, and redirect what you say. No book or videotape can replace your actual on-the-job experiences of teaching the fundamentals.

There's an old saying in sports that **practice makes perfect**. Later that saying was rephrased to state **perfect practice makes perfect**. The latter is

more valuable. We cannot overstate the importance of well-run practice sessions that stress the fundamentals. If the hitter has not been taught the fundamentals and does not have the

> **"It is not enough to emphasize the fundamentals only until the hitter no longer has any glaring deficiencies. The goal should be to make them an instinctive part of every player's game—so much so that the player does not have to think about them while in the game."**

rudiments of the swing, all the batting practice in the world will not help him realize his potential. It is not enough to emphasize the fundamentals only until the hitter no longer has any glaring deficiencies. The goal should be to make them an instinctive part of every player's game—so much so that the player does not have to think about them while in the game. He can correct his own deficiencies only by constantly reviewing how he is executing the fundamentals and basic techniques.

The difference between the great hitter and the good hitter is that the great hitter never gives up. When having difficulty, he does not respond by putting the bat back into the bat bag and going home. The great hitter develops the *three C's of hitting*: **C**onfidence, **C**oncentration, and **C**onsistency.

The road to successful hitting is not a short, simple trip. It is instead a long drawn-out journey that involves a lot of sweat and failure. For a young hitter to become an outstanding hitter, he must have not only natural physical abilities but, equally as important, a willingness to develop those abilities.

The structure of youth leagues and high school leagues forces players to be constantly funnelled through different teams, coaches, and organizations. In each new situation, the player is generally exposed to a new philosophy. In some cases, a hitter may have a coach who either does not follow through with the fundamentals or, in fact, may not know the fundamentals. In the early years, the most consistent and continual factor

> ### *The great hitter develops the three C's of hitting:*
>
> * Confidence,
> * Concentration,
> * Consistency.

in the child's progress is a parent. As time goes by, the hitter needs to move on beyond the parent's expertise to a more knowledgeable coach.

Eventually, however, the hitter must be able to help himself. If he doesn't understand what he needs to do not only to hit well, but to make adjustments when he's not hitting well, his progress will level off. *Each hitter is his own best hitting coach* because, after all, he is the only one who is there all the time. He must learn to evaluate and make determinations about his own hitting. This happens best if the hitter is solidly grounded in the fundamentals.

Those desiring more depth on advanced hitting skills might proceed to Chapter 9 and then return to Chapter 3.

# A Systematic Approach to Hitting

1. Bat selection

2. Depth and distance at the plate

3. Stance and balance

4. Grip on the bat

5. Box and bat angle

6. Inward turn

7. Stride

8. Swing

   a) *Focus the eyes*: Start on the eyes of the pitcher, and then move to the area of the ball at the release point.

   b) *Squish the bug*: Pivot the back foot and thrust the hips.

   c) *Slap the hands down*: Swing the bat in a slightly downward plane, through the ball.

   d) *Ike to Mike*: Keep the head down.

   e) *Follow-through*: Finish the swing.

## Quick Tips

- All hitters will be better if they use the standard grip.

- Hold the bat, but never squeeze it!

- It is much more important to learn how to hit correctly than to go for power. Let power evolve with time.

- Slow feet enhance fast hands, which is what the hitter wants. Quick feet get the hitter off balance and slow the hands, which the hitter does not want.

- Throw the head of the bat at the ball.

# CHAPTER THREE

# The Ten Most Common Hitting Mistakes and How to Correct Them

1. Stance/Stride
2. Grip
3. Box
4. Dead Stop Hitter
5. Back Foot Lockout
6. Bat Angle
7. Front Shoulder Early Release/ Quick Hip
8. Follow-Through
9. Tracking and Head Position
10. Fear of the Ball

Several hitting mistakes are made by players regardless of their age. In this chapter, we will cover the ten most common. Each mistake is followed by a discussion of possible corrections, though in some cases a correction may be no more than a restatement of a fundamental considered in Chapter 2. Reference is also made to certain corrective drills considered in Chapter 4.

## 1. Stance/Stride

### MISTAKES

*Stance.* Mistakes in stance are very common, but easily corrected. Often they are nothing more than the result of overcorrecting for a temporary slump or, as we prefer to call it, "an unfortunate period." The fact that even a good hitter faces failure about 70 percent of the time often leads to frequent changes or experiments with stance. For example, a hitter may hit well for a week with a particular stance. Suddenly he hits an unfortunate period, and his hitting falters. The first thing he changes, almost always, is his stance. If he had been using a slightly closed stance, he might switch to a slightly open stance. Then after another unfortunate period, he might adopt a parallel stance. When that doesn't work, he may cycle back to where he began. By the end of the year, the hitter may have run through five different stances without giving any of them a real chance to be proven effective or ineffective.

The most common and most detrimental flaw in the stance is angling the back foot outward (see Figure 1). Such an angle makes it nearly impossible to execute the pivoting of the back foot and the thrusting of the hips, that is, "squishing the bug."

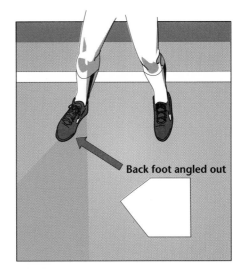

**Back foot angled out**

**FIGURE 1**
*Angling the back foot outward.*

## *For The Advanced Hitter*.....................................

*A common mistake of advanced hitters that is related to angling the back foot out is allowing their feet to inch toward or away from the plate—as much as one half inch per day. Over a seven-day period, this can amount to as much as 3 to 4 inches. It results mainly from pitching patterns. Perhaps one week the hitter is pitched low and away, so he may gradually inch closer to the plate. Eventually, he is unable to handle inside pitches. It is best for the hitter to let the pitcher come to him.*

A. Overstride.

B. Striding too close.

C. Striding away: stepping into the bucket.
**FIGURE 2**
*Mistakes in stride.*

*Stride.* Many young players struggle with their stride. Common mistakes vary from overstriding (taking too big a step with the front foot), to striding too close to the plate, to stepping away from the plate ("stepping into the bucket" or "bailing out"). See Figure 2 for examples.

> **"An incorrect stance is often nothing more than a hitter's inability to feel comfortable."**

## CORRECTIONS

*Stance.* An incorrect stance is often nothing more than a hitter's inability to feel comfortable. A hitter is far better off maintaining and developing one specific, workable stance than changing his stance four or five times during the season. The preferred stance for most young hitters positions the feet about shoulder width apart and parallel to a line from the pitcher through home plate (see Figure 3a). However, allow your hitters to experiment with a slightly open or slightly closed stance so long

**Note the toes pointing slightly in.**

*A.*

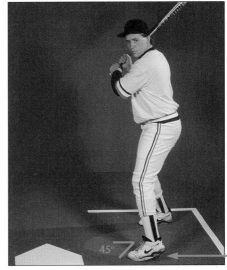

45°

**Proper stride**

*B.*

as the position is not extreme and doesn't hinder their swing.

Most important is that the stance be balanced. To test for balance, give the hitter a good shove in the chest or back. If he is positioned correctly, he will not be knocked off balance. Pointing the toes in slightly helps the hitter attain the proper *balance, stride,* and *hip rotation* in that order. If the hitter is comfortable with his stance, provided it is close to parallel and is balanced, then he should be encouraged to stay with it.

It is also important to keep reminding your players to avoid angling the back foot out and creeping toward the plate every time they step to the plate.

*Stride.* An improper stride—whether it is overstriding, striding too close, or striding away from the plate—can create more problems than the hitter can conceivably handle. Remind your young hitters to take a short stride of 4-8 inches at a 45-degree angle toward the plate (see Figure 3b). (As we mentioned in Chapter 2, the advanced hitter might not use the 45-degree angle.)

Two of the hitting drills discussed in Chapter 4, the *1-2-3* and the *spin hit,* are especially helpful for correcting an improper stride.

*Recommended drills*: Mirror, Spin Hit, 1-2-3, and Short Screen. (See Chapter 4.)

## 2. Grip

### MISTAKES

The hitter's grip helps determine how quickly the bat moves through the strike zone. In search of power, young hitters often mistakenly use the "choke grip" (see Figure 4a). A choke grip is defined by the way in which the hitter aligns his knuckles. The middle knuckles on the bottom hand align with the back knuckles on the top hand. If you carefully analyze hitters aged 16–18, you will find that at most only two out of 100 hitters are strong enough to move to the choke grip. Too many hitters who attempt such a grip either have not learned proper hitting techniques or are simply not prepared to be power hitters.

A choke grip forces greater use of muscles in the chest, shoulders, and back, and less use of those in the hands, wrists, and arms that allow for greater speed and quickness in release of the head of the bat through the strike zone. A choke grip also creates a negative effect of "sweeping" the bat through the strike zone instead of a positive effect of "throwing" the bat through the zone. Finally, a choke grip also causes an uppercut in the swing that leads to pop-ups or missed swings. Some hitters make this grip even worse by wrapping the bat deep into the palm of the hand, resulting not only in decreased bat quickness and speed, but often badly bruised hands.

### CORRECTIONS

No matter which grip is used, it should be in the fingers, not the palms. The choke grip should be considered *only* after the hitter has learned good hitting fundamentals and has a firm indication that he can be a power hitter. The suggested grip for virtually all hitters is the *standard grip*. The key to this grip is aligning the middle knuckles on both hands and keeping the bat in the fingers and not the palms of the hands (see Figure 4b). The standard grip enhances the use of the hitter's forearms, wrists, hands, and fingers, helping to attain quickness with the head of the bat (see Figure 4c).

Often a hitter will come to you with a grip other than the standard simply because he has been poorly taught by his former coaches. The key then is to identify what grip he has and convince him to change to a standard grip, out in the fingers, for an exten-

"The key to the standard grip is getting the bat out into the fingers with the middle knuckles aligned."

A. The choke grip.

B. The standard grip.

FIGURE 4       C. Positioning the standard grip.

**Carl Yastrzemski**

sive period of time. He may resist you because it won't "feel right" immediately, but given time, it will feel comfortable for most hitters.

*Recommended drills:* Mirror. (See Chapter 4.)

## 3. Box

### MISTAKES

Your goal as a coach is to maximize the hitter's ability by eliminating as many mistakes as possible. One common error to watch for is incorrect positioning of the hands and arms. It is important to be sure that the hitter forms a proper "box," as we discussed in Chapter 2. The hands and arms need to remain in an area that will allow the greatest opportunity for success. They should not be too high or too low, and they should not be allowed to move back with the inward turn other than by moving along with the body. Examples of a proper box and improper boxes are shown in Figure 5.

Many of you may remember Reggie Smith and Carl Yastrzemski, who played together for the Boston Red Sox. Each of these great hitters held

his bat high above his head with the arms almost straight, as shown in Figure 5(b). Julio Franco of the Texas Rangers is a successful hitter who holds his bat with his hands wrapped behind his head. An example of such a hitter is shown in Figure 5(c). Your players may recall other examples. Be sure to point out to them, however, that these players are *exceptions* to the rule. In fact, prior to impact, all return their hands and arms to a fundamentally sound position.

YOU CAN TEACH HITTING

FIGURE 5

*A. A proper box.*

*B. An improper box:*
*The hands and arms are too high.*

*C. An improper box:*
*The hands are wrapped behind the head.*

*D. An improper box:*
*The hands and arms are too low.*

*Julio Franco*

*Jose Canseco*

Wide World Photos

Wide World Photos

Another common error is moving the hands down in what is called a "hitch." Dropping the hands down when the ball is traveling toward the hitter generally creates a late swing, especially on hard fastballs up in the strike zone. Some great hitters, such as Hall-of-Famer Hank Aaron and present-day players Jose Canseco and Kevin Mitchell, have such a hitch. They start the act early, however, and thus are able to return their hands close to the proper location before the ball reaches the hitting area. A hitch is not recommended because it is very difficult to time and to master.

## For The Advanced Hitter...........................................

*Correcting a hitch in an advanced hitter can be a very challenging task because that hitch is probably an instinctive part of his batting stroke. One way to do so, however, is to move the hitter's hands further down as close as possible to the bottom of the hitch. Then have him begin his swing from that position.*

*Another method is to let the batter hitch, but work with him to hitch earlier—that is, learn to time it to the pitcher's windup so that the hands get back up close to a proper position in time for the swing. Often all you can do with an advanced hitter, unfortunately, is help him minimize the hitch.*

## CORRECTIONS

A proper box eliminates most of the potential hitting mistakes. The proper box runs across the top of the shoulders, down the front arm, across the bottom forearm, and then up the back arm. In particular, be sure that the hitter does not keep his back elbow up. That elbow should be down, so that it can form the other side of a proper box. It should also be comfortable but not too close to the body.

You might observe a hitter stretching the box by moving the hands either back or down on the inward turn or stride. When they move, the hands should roll straight back, but with the body and not in an exaggerated manner. Be sure the box stays intact through the hitter's stance and stride.

To help a younger hitter correct a hitch, have him think of moving the hands back by virtue of being connected with the body. In other words, the inward turn takes the hands back. The hands do not go back by themselves, but with the body as it makes the inward turn. Carried out in this manner, the inward turn might be thought of as a "correct hitch."

*Recommended drills*: Mirror, Fence, Short Screen, and Spin Hit. (See Chapter 4.)

## 4. Dead Stop Hitter

### MISTAKE

When the ball is released from the pitcher's hand, a **dead stop hitter** makes absolutely no movement backward before he moves forward to propel himself into his swing. The hitter's first movement goes forward or doesn't go anywhere. If the first movement is forward, it could be the front

## *For The Advanced Hitter*.....................

A young dead stop hitter who drifts forward is more susceptible to hard pitches, inside pitches, and soft pitches. The older, more advanced dead stop hitter is more susceptible to hard pitches, particularly high and inside pitches, but not soft pitches.

foot or the hands. This weakens his effectiveness in two ways. One, from the very start it takes away some of his strength. He is either like a coiled spring, with no way to uncoil, or a spring that has uncoiled prematurely. The hitter either hasn't dissipated his strength or has none to dissipate. Second, the average dead stop hitter, unless he is exceptionally strong, is a better middle-speed hitter and *not* a good fastball hitter.

## CORRECTION

A critical problem occurs for the hitter when the pitcher's speed differs greatly between the fastball and the off-speed pitch. When a dead stop hitter encounters pitches that vary from 83 mph to 60 mph, he is in trouble. Although he gears up to hit a fastball

with every pitch, as well he should, his hands either won't have moved at all or will have started forward as though a fastball had, in fact, been thrown.

To correct this mistake, a dead stop hitter must create an **inward turn**—that is, he must move backward before he moves forward. This backward movement is crucial for two reasons:

1. It helps the hitter gather strength, thus providing extra power; and

2. It provides the hitter with the ability to time pitches.

**FIGURE 6**
*A correct inward turn.*

YOU CAN TEACH HITTING

As we mentioned earlier, to attain an inward turn the hitter must remember: "When the pitcher shows you his hip pocket, show him yours!" He does this by tucking either his front knee, front hip, front shoulder, or some combination of all three. What the hitter achieves is a slight roll of the hands backward, no more than 3 inches. This movement should be connected to and result from movement of the front half of the body. When the knee, hip, or shoulder tucks, the hands should roll back at the same time (see Figure 6).

*Recommended drills*: 1-2-3-4, Short Screen, and Mirror. ( See Chapter 4.)

## 5. Back Foot Lockout

### MISTAKE

A common mistake for young hitters is **back foot lockout**. This can vary from not rotating up on the back foot at all, to rotating only a little bit, to rotating late. Back foot lockout occurs exactly the way it sounds. When the hitter executes his swing, he gets no rotation on the back foot and no hip thrust, thus causing three difficulties.

First, back foot lockout forces a loop in the hitter's swing. With no thrust or rotation of the hips, the hitter pulls the back shoulder down slightly, making the shoulders uneven from the beginning. Even a swing that is outstanding in all other aspects results in a slight uppercut and is not level.

Second, the lack of hip thrust prevents the hitter from effectively using his lower body. Since about 70 percent of total body strength is from the waist down, this costs him valuable power (see Figure 7).

Third, when the hitter does not roll up and rotate on the back foot ("squish the bug"), any pitch on the outside third of the plate is physically impos-

"Back foot lockout is far and away the most common mistake made by hitters!"

sible to reach unless the hitter is standing right on top of the plate. This would in turn, however, render him susceptible to an inside pitch. A back foot lockout hitter tends to slice the ball away (to the right for a right-handed hitter).

## CORRECTION

Although back foot lockout is far and away the most common mistake made by hitters, it is dealt with the *least* by coaches! Coaches generally react by moving the hitter closer to the plate or adjusting something that is completely irrelevant. They miss the point of getting the hitter to roll up on the back foot and thrust the hips.

To correct the problem of back foot lockout, it is important to take a methodical approach with your players. It involves a lot of practice both at the field and at home. Although it might be easy for your young hitters to visualize squishing the bug, it might be difficult for them to execute.

Eliminating back foot lockout involves what is called *muscle memory*—that is, training the muscles to react in a special way through repetition without conscious thought. Just as a computer must be programmed to operate correctly, a hitter's muscle memory must be programmed to operate in a specific way at a certain time.

An 86-mph average major league fastball allows a hitter only 0.4 second to execute the swing from the time the ball leaves the pitcher's hand. It takes 0.2 second for the hitter to see the ball and to determine whether he's going to swing. This leaves only 0.2 second to actually execute the swing. If the hitter has not *programmed* his muscle memory to carry out the fundamentals of a proper swing—in particular, rolling up on the back foot and thrusting the hips—his chances of performing the swing successfully are very slim. If the hitter does hit the ball successfully without the proper fundamentals, it's due to sheer luck or tremendous athletic ability. You don't want a hitter to rely only on these.

*Each and every day*, not just Monday, Wednesday, and Saturday, schedule three minutes for the following corrective procedure. Have the hitter place the bat behind his back, resting it on his waistline (see Figures 8a and 8b). With his hands behind the bat in a firm grip, he then gets in his stance, takes his stride, and stops. Once he

**FIGURE 8**
*The bat behind-the-back drill.*

**A. Start of the drill for the right-handed hitter.**

**B. Completion of the drill for the right-handed hitter.**

**C. Start of the drill for the left-handed hitter.**

**D. Completion of the drill for the left-handed hitter.**

has stopped, he takes his right hand, if right-handed, and forcefully pulls the bat around his waist. The idea is to pull hard. When he does so, he will roll up on the back foot. Repeating this drill 20 times per day will take only about three minutes and will go a long way toward correcting back foot lockout. A good mental image for your players is to think of "hitting the ball with the back hip" when they are carrying out this drill.

The drill is shown for a left-handed batter in Figures 8(c) and 8(d). Note that the drill can also be done by bracing the bat in the forearms just above the wrists.

The importance of this drill is that the hitter will begin to program his hips and back foot to operate without conscious thought. If he goes to the plate in the middle of the game and tries to physically think about rolling up on the back foot and thrusting the hips, one result is virtually guaranteed: The ball will be past the hitter, in the catcher's mitt, and halfway back to the pitcher's mound before he even decides what he's going to do! When a hitter goes to the plate, he has 0.4 second to do two things: (1) determine if the pitch is a good one to hit (see if it's

one he feels he can hit); and (2) hit the ball hard. This does not leave him time to think about all the mechanics of a good swing.

*Recommended drills:* Bat Behind the Back, Spin Hit, Mirror, 1-2-3, and Hip Thrust. (See Chapter 4.)

# 6. Bat Angle

### MISTAKE

The hitter can determine the ease with which his bat transfers into the strike zone just by the way he holds it. Many problems are caused by nervous habits, such as excessive movement of the bat, which a hitter may use to help him relax. In truth, excessive movement is better than no movement, because a bat held stationary feels heavier than a bat that is moving. Excessive movement, however, results in a poor bat angle, and *improper bat angle* is a common error.

Many young hitters hold the bat straight up at a 90-degree angle (see Figure 9). Even a strong hitter, however, will have trouble with this bat angle. It is important to encourage hitters to use the 45-degree angle. Why? Because eventually the bat must

**FIGURE 9**

**A. Suggested: the 45-degree bat angle.**

**B. Not suggested: the 90-degree bat angle.**

be in the same plane as the ball in order to hit it, so why not begin the swing closer to that plane? The 45-degree angle makes it easier for the hitter to lay the bat down level in the strike zone.

Some hitters also tend to wrap the bat around the head (see Figure 10). This tactic is unfortunately part of some modern batting theories, but not one we support. In wrapping the bat, the hitter elongates the swing, making it a lot slower. This in turn forces him to start his swing sooner, allowing him less time to identify and react to off-speed pitches. It is common for hitters to compensate for this by moving the hands forward for a quicker swing. Such a hitter runs the risk, however, of making himself vulnerable to offspeed pitches and hard fastballs up in the strike zone.

Bat wrapped behind head

**FIGURE 10**
**Improper bat angle: The bat is wrapped behind the head.**

Ryne Sandberg taking a proper stride with a proper bat angle.

## CORRECTION

Correcting a mistake in bat angle is simple in theory, but somewhat difficult in practice, so encourage young hitters to begin with the recommended 45-degree angle.

Some hitters tend to change the bat angle as the pitch approaches. Often such a change is merely a nervous habit. It may also occur in an attempt to make the inward turn. The hitter should learn to achieve this, however, by tucking the front shoulder, hip, knee, or some combination of all three, *not* by changing the bat angle.

With a proper 45-degree bat angle, the hitter can transfer the bat into the hitting zone more easily. This angle also allows him to make better and more consistent contact, since the 90-degree angle forces a loop into his swing. The best way to correct a bat-angle error is to carefully observe the hitter as he takes his swings. A hitter might also catch his own error by analyzing his swing in a mirror or on a videotape.

*Recommended drills*: Mirror, Fence, Spin Hit, Chair, and Short Screen. (See Chapter 4.)

# 7. Front Shoulder Early Release/Quick Hip

## MISTAKE

The **_front shoulder early release_** or **_quick hip_** causes more batting slumps than any mistake other than merely not seeing the ball. The result of releasing the front hip and shoulder before the ball reaches the hitter causes four problems:

1. The hitter is very vulnerable to an offspeed pitch.

2. The hitter is more vulnerable to pitches that are out over the plate, toward the outside corner.

3. The hitter finds it difficult to hit balls well, particularly to the opposite field.

4. If the ball is pulled (to the left side for a right-handed hitter), it is highly probable that it will be a foul ball.

The front shoulder early release or quick hip is directly related to back foot lockout. The back foot can't rotate effectively if the front shoulder and/or hip release too quickly. When a hitter does not operate the back foot and hips properly, he cuts off at least

Front hip and shoulder released too early

**FIGURE 11**
**_Front shoulder early release._**

half of his total body strength. He might then subconsciously compensate for this loss of quickness by not rotating. In other words, the front shoulder early release or quick hip is generally a compensation for a back foot that doesn't do its job (see Figure 11). Although the hitter may make contact, it will probably be off the end of the bat, because an early release of the front shoulder will pull the bat in toward the hitter and away from the pitch.

## CORRECTION

It would seem that front shoulder early release or quick hip could be corrected by working on the back foot. But the correction of the back foot alone may not solve the problem of the front shoulder. Even if the hitter does his 20 repetitions a day in order to correct back foot lockout, his front shoulder will typically continue to fly open.

The first step to correction is to show a young hitter exactly what this mistake will do to his swing. Begin by getting in your stance with a bat. Then, as you begin to swing, in slow motion allow the front shoulder and/or front hip to leave first. Shortly thereafter, the back foot will start to rotate. What you want the hitter to notice is that your upper body is now so open, in order to extend your hands and get your arms straight with a straight line down the front arm all the way through the bat, the bat angle will be pointing almost directly toward the pitcher. In other words, if the hitter gets an inside pitch, he will have almost no bat with which to hit. Thus he will hit or tap almost every ball off the end of the bat. An outside pitch, at this point, is almost physically impossible to hit.

Next, begin the following hitting drill. Ask the hitter to let the first two or three pitches go by while merely pointing his front shoulder at the ball. On the next pitch, tell him to keep the front shoulder in as long as possible and then swing. Then have him hit two balls to the opposite field. He should point his front shoulder at the ball, keep it there as long as possible, and then lead with his back foot and hip, not with his front shoulder. The goal is for the front shoulder to stay in as long as possible and then explode at the last second. This "power explosion" must come with the back foot and the hips, not the front shoulder.

*Recommended drills:* Now, Overload, Fence, Spin Hit, 1-2-3, and Mirror. (See Chapter 4.)

## 8. *Follow-Through*

### MISTAKE

As in virtually every sport, good follow-through in baseball will spell the difference between a poor hitter and a successful one. A mistake in ***follow-through,*** seen more with younger players than with older players, is a failure to continue the swing to its completion, with the bat around the

**FIGURE 12**     *A. Completed follow-through.*     *B. Poor follow-through.*

hitter's front shoulder. Many hitters with this difficulty either lack aggressiveness in their swing or use an incorrect grip. If they have the bat choked in the palm, not in the fingers, the wrists cannot move freely. Thus an incomplete follow-through can be caused by tension in the swing and hitting *at* the ball rather than *through* the ball.

If a hitter stops his bat out in front without completing his follow-through, where did he start slowing down? See Figure 12(b). Most often, the hitter will tell you that he began slowing down at the point of contact.

It stands to reason that that's exactly what he does not want! He wants to make sure that when he starts his swing, he is inside the ball with the knob pointing at the pitch. Then he accelerates his hands to the ball, not by rolling the wrists prematurely, but by driving through the ball. Such actions translate to building speed through the swing.

It is surprising how many young hitters are insecure about hitting a small round ball with a small round bat! The hitter may slow down, thinking his aim will be more certain. This defeats the purpose of the swing.

## CORRECTION

It is important to keep reminding your players, "Follow through and finish the swing!" The hitter should not back off at any point in the swing. This may seem to be a simple solution but for many hitters the correction is quite a battle.

A complete follow-through occurs when the hitter finishes the swing with the bat out and away from the front shoulder. Ask your hitters to think of this as throwing at a target—that is, they want to make contact with the ball and then throw the ball out off the bat. The best way to accomplish this is through repetitive work while continually reminding the hitter if his follow-through is correct or incorrect. Keep stressing, "Follow through and finish the swing." (See Figure 12.)

Also, observe the way in which the hitter is holding his hands when he does not follow through. Make sure he is using the standard grip. An incorrect grip can prohibit a good follow-through. In a good swing, the hitter starts the swing short, hits through the ball, and finishes long to avoid cutting off the swing!

A mental image that you can use with hitters to teach follow-through is to have them think of two balls being pitched, one about 6 to 8 inches behind the other. The goal of the hitter is to hit through the first ball in order to attack the second ball.

**"In a good swing, the hitter starts the swing short, hits through the ball, and finishes long to avoid cutting off the swing!"**

Once a hitter gets a feel for how hard and well he can hit the ball with a correct follow-through, he typically makes a quick correction. Hitting the ball hard and getting a double into left center field is much more fun than lining out to the shortstop!

*Recommended drills:* Fence, One Hand, Spin Hit, Mirror, and Short Screen. (See Chapter 4.)

# 9. Tracking and Head Position

## MISTAKES

Another common hitting mistake is improper ***tracking and head position***. When the hitter is not tracking the ball properly, he is not seeing the ball all the way from the release point of the pitcher to the hitting area in front of the plate. This makes the hitter swing late on fastballs and early on breaking balls.

A related mistake is not keeping the head down on the ball with the chin down on the chest at the point of contact. This error prevents the activation of muscles in the neck, from the neck to the shoulder, in the shoulder, and down the sides in the back and the tricep muscles. The swing is always more powerful when the hitter keeps his head down!

**FIGURE 13**
*Correcting mistakes in tracking and head position.*

*A. Focus on the pitcher's eyes.*

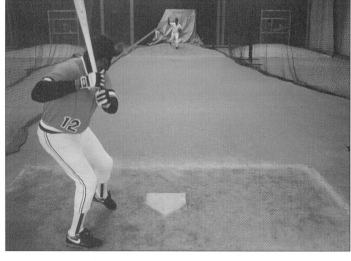

*B. Move to the area of the ball at the release point.*

## CORRECTIONS

To help correct this difficulty, suggest that the hitter choose a focal point on the pitcher—perhaps the lettering on his cap or his eyes. As the pitcher brings his arm forward, the hitter then moves his eye to the area of the ball at the release point. He should follow the ball all the way, with his eyes tracking down with the ball into the hitting area. The head stays down, with the chin close to the chest at the point of contact (see "Ike to Mike," discussed in the systematic approach to hitting in Chapter 2).

Looking at the focal points with both eyes, not allowing the head to tilt, the hitter keeps his eyes straight ahead and parallel to the front shoulder. See Figure 13.

# 10. Fear of the Ball

## MISTAKE

Although technically not a mistake, fear of the ball is a common problem in younger hitters. They stand at the plate more concerned with avoiding a pitch than with carrying out proper fundamentals. Fear of the ball is related to improper tracking of the ball from the release point and not knowing how to avoid getting hit by the pitch or minimizing the pain of being hit.

## CORRECTION

Correct tracking and head position, as we just discussed, can help in eliminating fear of the ball. If the hitter tracks the ball properly, he has a much better chance of moving out of the way, if necessary.

Equally important is to teach young hitters how to get out of the way of the ball in a proper manner. If he senses that he is about to be hit by a pitch, the hitter should turn the front shoulder and body inward toward the catcher (see Figure 14). If the hitter is doing his inward turn correctly, the rotation is more easily accomplished. Turning completely toward the catcher ensures that if he does get hit, it will be in the least vulnerable parts of the body—the back, buttocks, or back of the legs. Dropping the bat to the ground while turning also protects the bat from being hit by the pitch, thus preventing an unnecessary foul strike.

Fear of the ball can also be minimized by having players concentrate on watching the ball longer when play-

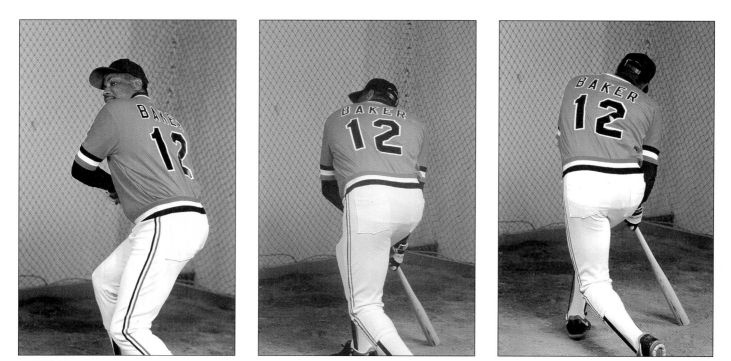

**FIGURE 14**
*The proper way to avoid being hit by a pitch.*

ing catch with another player. The hitter watches the ball from the release point in the same way that he would watch a pitch. Another method is to have the hitter stand at the plate and tell him that you are going to attemp to hit him. Then using tennis balls, throw some pitches, most but not all of which are at the player. He will first discover that most of the time he can indeed avoid being hit. At the same time, he can practice the proper method of getting out of the way.

The important thing to remember is that learning both how to track the ball and how to get out of the way, if necessary, will eventually eliminate fear of the ball. This in turn frees the hitter to concentrate on the fundamentals when he steps to the plate.

# CHAPTER FOUR

# Hitting Drills

Drill  #1:   Fence Drill

Drill  #2:   One-Hand Drill

Drill  #3:   Right/Left/Middle

Drill  #4:   1-2-3-4 Drill

Drill  #5:   Soft-Toss Breaker

Drill  #6:   Bat Behind the Back

Drill  #7:   Overload Drill

Drill  #8:   Spin Hit

Drill  #9:   Game Time

Drill #10:   Low Pitch

Drill #11:   High Pitch

Drill #12:   Mirror Drill

Drill #13:   Short Screen

Drill #14:   Now Drill

Drill #15:   1-2-3 Drill

Drill #16:   Chair Drill

Drill #17:   Hip Thrust

Drill #18:   Iso Bat

Drill #19:   Counts and Situations

Drill #20:   Up and Down

This chapter describes 20 drills that we have found successful in working with hundreds of hitters at various levels of ability. Each drill is designed to correct certain common mistakes covered in Chapter 3 or to deal with a special need of a particular player. Keep in mind that you may not need all 20 drills for all players. Although the intent is to teach the same basic hitting fundamentals to all young hitters, the teaching philosophy should always allow for differences. Choosing appropriate drills allows a coach to handle the individual problems and meet the special needs of each hitter. The goal is to customize hitting instruction for each player.

A few drills, such as the soft-toss breaker and short screen, require the use of an L-screen or a short screen. If these are not available, the drill can be carried out with whiffle balls.

There are two keys to utilizing each hitting drill:

1. Determine which drill is appropriate for which problem. To help you do so, we discuss with each drill which mistakes, if any, from Chapter 3 are being corrected or which special need is being cov-

ered. Also included is appropriateness by age level.

2. Ensure that the drill is done correctly.

At the end of the chapter, you will also find a reference table reiterating each drill and, if appropriate, the common mistakes it can be used to correct. In all these drills, we assume that the hitter has warmed up properly with appropriate stretching exercises.

# DRILL #1
## *Fence Drill*
### (age 13 and older)

The **fence drill** is beneficial for those hitters who tend to extend the hands and arms too quickly in their swing. An inherent problem in the stroke, such as an improper grip, can cause a hitter to sweep the bat through the strike zone and extend the hands and arms too quickly. The result is that he finds it very difficult to hit an inside pitch. This mistake also decreases bat velocity. The hitter needs to keep his hands in close to his body a bit longer before eventually exploding the hips and extending the arms. The goal of the drill is to create a fundamentally correct swing.

The fence drill can also be used effectively to teach players to hit the ball to the opposite field. This is important for a hit and run, where the goal is to hit a ground ball to the opposite field. The hitter will actually be leading with his hands and the bat head will trail the knob until the hitter is ready to throw the bat head, extend his arms, and swing down and through the ball in a proper manner. The fence drill teaches a hitter to stay inside the ball. Done correctly, it teaches more of an inside-out stroke rather than an outside-in stroke.

In setting up this drill, you will need some type of a solid surface, such as a chain link fence, that is at least six feet tall so that it's above the head of the hitter. A backstop, concrete wall, or brick wall will also work, but a freestanding, hanging net will not.

Position the player with his feet in a parallel stance about a foot (or a foot and a half, depending on his size) away from the fence (see Figure 1). To check for the appropriate distance, the hitter should reach out with his back arm and touch the wall. If he is in the correct position, his arm will be slightly bent. If his arm is completely straight, he is probably too far away.

**FIGURE 1**
*#1: The fence drill.*

*A. Beginning the drill.*

*B. Swinging through.*

*C. Completing the drill.*

The object of this drill is to take as normal a cut as possible without making contact with the fence. It is important to go through the drill very slowly for the first several repetitions. Have the hitter go into a slow-motion stroke before taking a full cut. This will prevent him from being afraid of the fence when he is swinging. If the drill is done incorrectly, the hitter will hit the fence and get immediate, clear feedback.

The hitter should take a parallel stride. The key to the drill is to keep the bat head above the back shoulder, not allowing it to drop down beside the shoulder until the appropriate time. If it does, the bat will make contact with the fence as the hitter opens his hips to swing. If the hitter keeps the bat above his shoulder, with his hands in fairly close to his body, and allows his back foot to begin first, he can execute the drill correctly. In other words, if he allows his back foot to open the upper body and prepare him to swing, he will execute the drill. As he takes a parallel stride, he should open up with the back foot and thrust the hips ("squish the bug"). Then he rotates the hips, keeping the bat head above the back shoulder. Once open, away from the fence, he extends his arms and finishes the swing down and through the ball in the proper manner.

When the hitter is able to do this successfully, it looks very natural. But at first appearance, it's an intimidating drill and can be difficult to execute if the hitter isn't shown how to do so properly. Be careful not to overdo the drill. Try 5 to 7 repetitions per day for hitters who extend their arms too early.

YOU CAN TEACH HITTING

# DRILL #2
## *One-Hand Drill*
### (age 10 and older)

The **one-hand drill** is very effective in building the confidence of young hitters, who are generally insecure about their hitting ability. It does so by showing them that they can hit the ball if they emphasize a slightly downward swing ("slap the hands down").

To carry out the one-hand drill, use a short screen and have the hitter use a lighter or shorter bat to prevent wrist and shoulder injury. Throw from one knee to the hitter from a distance of about 20 or 30 feet. The hitter either stands or gets down on his back knee.

To work on the bottom hand, have the hitter choke his bottom hand up to the top of the tape or grip and place his top hand and arm across his chest (see Figure 2a).

To work on the top hand, have him take his top hand and choke it up at the top of the tape. Then have him place his bottom hand and arm across his chest (see Figure 2b), which will help him pull his hips through the swing.

Top hand and arm placed across chest

Bottom hand at top of tape or leather grip

**A. Emphasizing the bottom hand.**

Top hand at top of tape or leather grip

Bottom hand and arm placed across chest

**B. Emphasizing the top hand.**

**FIGURE 2**
**#2: The one-hand drill.**

Have the hitter position the bat as though he were hitting with two hands and then begin throwing him pitches. The object is to make good contact, hitting line drives or ground balls. Begin with the hitter choked up a bit on the bat. Continue to have him make contact and, as he gets more comfortable, have him move his hands down on the bat to his normal position. Once he has accomplished the goal of making contact at that point, he can put both hands back on the bat.

**"THE BOTTOM HAND IS CONSIDERED THE POWER HAND."**

The one-hand drill allows the hitter to keep the bottom hand fairly close to his body while working on good extension and bat speed. The bottom hand is considered the "power" hand. In a proper swing, the bottom hand must be on course with the ball first. Then the top hand hits through the ball and the bottom hand continues the follow-through. You will likely need to work on the bottom hand more than the top, but neither hand should be taught to excess.

## DRILL #3
## *Right/Left/Middle*
### (age 13 and older)

At some point in the development of the fundamentals of the hitter's swing (usually at age 13 and older), you will see the need to progress to the next level of instruction. At that point each hitter should work daily on hitting the ball to the right, to the left, and up the middle—hence, the *right/left/middle drill.* Although there is actually more room to hit the ball up the middle, that part of the field is often ignored. Yes, the pitcher fields the middle, but generally he has less reaction time and, at higher levels, is not as adept defensively as the other infielders.

For a right-handed hitter, the *pull* field is left field between the third-base line and the shortstop out to the fence. The *opposite* field is right field between the first-base line and the second baseman out to the fence. The *middle* field is between the shortstop and second baseman out to the fence between left center field and right center field. For the left-handed batter, the right side is the pull field and the left side is the opposite field. See Figure 3.

FIGURE 3

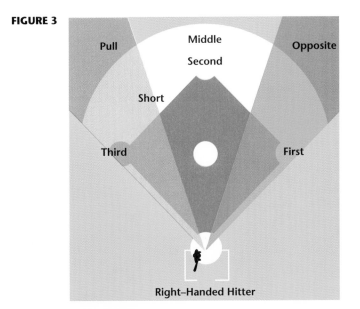

Right–Handed Hitter

Start by having the hitter hit three pitches to the opposite field, then three pitches to the pull field, and then three pitches up the middle. Then repeat the cycle. We suggest using three pitches in order to produce the following thought process:

1. mistake,
2. correction, and
3. reinforcement.

Although the goal for the hitter is, of course, to connect with the first swing, often it does not happen that way. If, in fact, he makes a mistake

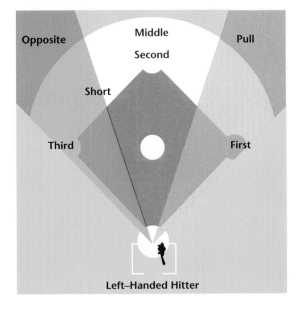

Left–Handed Hitter

## Keys to Hitting the Ball to the Opposite Field

- Rotating the back foot ("squishing the bug")
- Allowing the top hand to play an aggressive role in the swing
- Keeping the head down on the ball
- Waiting on the ball and staying balanced
- Using the legs, that is, keeping the front leg bent and driving through the ball with both legs
- Staying inside the ball.

with the first swing, you should correct the problem with the second swing and reinforce the correction on the third pitch.

Using the legs keeps the bat angle on top of the ball since most pitches are low in the strike zone. Thinking about using the legs also reminds us to bend the knees. On a normal swing, the batter hits off a firm front leg.

## DRILL #4
## *1-2-3-4 Drill*
### (age 10 and older)

The *1-2-3-4 drill* is designed for hitters who have difficulty attaining an inward turn. In other words, they're not going back before going forward. They are not coiling like a jack-in-the-box, gathering strength, and then uncoiling. In general, the dead stop hitter's problem begins with the first movement, which is straight forward. Often older hitters, especially those who are not handling breaking balls very well, are in front of nearly every pitch. Generally, this problem has to do with not making an inward turn.

To correct this problem, it is important to break down the actual stance and inward turn into a four-step process. By doing so, you can isolate and concentrate on the hitter's specific problems and simplify the correction. Position the hitter in his stance and have him begin moving back and forth. All he needs to do is lift his heels off the ground one at a time, shifting his weight from one side to the other in a bit of a rhythm. He's actually moving back and forth from the pitcher to the catcher (see Figure 4). In other words, he

1. rocks toward the pitcher, then
2. toward the catcher, then
3. toward the pitcher, and then
4. toward the catcher (to coil and explode into the swing).

The motion is not an exaggerated one. In fact, it's very slight. The goal of this drill is to attain some rhythm and movement, making an inward turn easier. It is better to have some rhythm and movement than none at all. As the hitter rocks back and forth, call the 1-2-3-4 count. That is, as he rocks forward, call "1." As he rocks back, call "2." As he rocks forward again, it's "3," and as he rocks back, it's "4." In this manner, the hitter makes the inward turn. You want the hitter to move his hands back just a

**FIGURE 4**
*#4: The 1-2-3-4 drill.*

*A. Step 1: Rock forward.*

*B. Step 2: Rock back.*

*C. Step 3: Rock forward.*

*D. Step 4: Rock back.*

bit, but not in a manner distinct from the rest of the body.

On the "4" count, the hitter rocks the hands and swings, forcing him to get his inward turn. The front half of the body—that is, the front knee, the front hip, and the front shoulder— should do the rocking of the hands for the hitter. If you are throwing balls to the hitter from either a regulation distance or a short screen, begin throwing on the "3" count. As the hitter rolls back for "4," the ball will then be on its way and the timing will be just about right.

Young hitters tend to have a problem with this drill when they get away from the rocking motion and lose their rhythm. The rhythm actually gives them an opportunity to time pitches. Timing is so very important as the hitters get older and face off-speed pitches with regularity.

## DRILL #5
## *Soft-Toss Breaker*
## (age 15 and older)

The **soft-toss breaker drill** is designed primarily for older hitters who will see breaking pitches. It forces the hitter to center his weight in the mid-

**FIGURE 5**
*#5: The soft-toss breaker.*

dle of his body, keep his hands back, and delay the stroke as long as possible. The drill is executed with the hitter standing in front of an open field or a soft-toss screen or net. A backstop can also be used if a net or screen isn't available. What is important is that the hitter be able to take a full cut and drive the ball.

In a general soft-toss drill, the person feeding the ball stands 5 to 6 feet away and behind the hitter in back of the other batting box. He then tosses the ball to the hitter, who hits it into a screen. The soft-toss breaker drill is similar to a regular soft toss, but the

"feeder" stands about three steps directly behind the hitter and then moves about two steps to the hitter's right. In other words, the ball comes from an angle behind the hitter (see Figure 5). The feeder then gets down on one knee and feeds pitches from behind so that the ball comes up through the strike zone. This forces the hitter to keep his hands back until the last possible second. Once the hitter sees the ball out of the corner of his eye, he swings through the hitting zone and drives the ball into the screen or the field. The hitter should be careful not to turn his head and look at the person who is feeding, but

A. Beginning the drill.

B. Completing the drill.

FIGURE 6
#6: The bat-behind-the-back drill.

rather keep his eyes focused on the hitting zone.

# DRILL #6
## *Bat Behind the Back*
### (age 8 and older)

The **bat-behind-the-back drill** is a necessity for nearly all hitters, but it is particularly important for young players, who are just beginning to develop their fundamental skills. Assuming, as always, that he has warmed up to avoid pulled muscles, the hitter gets into his regular stance and places the bat behind his back either right on the belt or on the belt line of his baseball pants. Then he puts his hands on the back side of the bat so that he can pull hard while executing the drill.

This particular drill can be done either with or without a stride. If no stride is used, the hitter takes a position as though he has finished his stride. Then with his right hand (for a right-handed hitter; or with his left hand for a left-handed hitter), he pulls the bat around the back with the head of the bat toward the pitcher. At the same time, he rolls up on the back foot and squishes the bug (see Figure 6).

The hitter *strides*, if desired, and *pulls*. He uses the bat to help his hips drive through, making sure at the same time to complete the rotation on the back foot. This is an excellent drill for improving the hitter's hip quickness, for developing the habit of squishing the bug with every swing, and for quickening the swing, particularly on inside pitches.

This drill should be part of *every* hitter's daily routine. Repetitions should involve 15 to 20 per day for the older hitters and 5 to 10 per day for the younger hitters. Although the drill takes only two to three minutes to complete, the benefits reaped are immeasurable.

# DRILL #7
## *Overload Drill*
## (age 15 and older)

The **overload drill** is a higher-level drill designed for the advanced hitter who has a severe problem with front shoulder early release/quick hip.

The drill is a four-step process for the player. In **step 1**, the hitter stands with his back foot about 4 to 6 inches from the plate. His front foot will be parallel to the other foot in a line perpendicular to the plate (see Figure 7a). Standing with his chest facing the pitcher, he is then fed pitches. From this stance, the hitter is not allowed to move his feet as he swings. He can swivel his hips around to face the plate and turn his front shoulder in pointing it at the pitcher, but he cannot move his feet. In this first step of the overload drill, there is no stride involved and there is also no rolling up on the back foot.

The focus is to teach the hitter how to keep his front shoulder in as long as possible, keep his head down, and hit the ball as hard as he can on a line or on the ground to the opposite field. Especially useful for hitters who consistently come open with their front shoulders and pull their heads up off the ball, this drill forces them to stay down. Then beginning with the stance in the first step, the hitter is systematically moved back toward a regular stance, stride, and swing.

Some hitters can't master step 1 at first. It may take them a week or longer to execute it. It is important, however, to be sure that they have mastered step 1 before proceeding to the next steps.

In **step 2**, the hitter leaves the back foot exactly where it was, but rotates it

FIGURE 7
#7: The overload drill.

Back foot 4–6 inches from plate.

Front foot parallel to other foot with chest facing pitcher.

**A. Step 1: swing from a perpendicular position.**

Back foot stays exactly where it was.

Front foot, which was parallel to back foot, is moved to an angle up first-base line for left-handed hitter and up third-base line for right-handed hitter.

**B. Step 2: swing with the front foot up the base line.**

**C. Step 3: spin hit.**

**D. Step 4: normal swing.**

slightly toward the catcher. The front foot, which was parallel to the back foot, is moved to an angle either up the first-base line for a left-handed hitter or up the third-base line for a right-handed hitter (see Figure 7b). Once again the hitter is not allowed to move his feet. He is to work completely with the upper body. He should point the shoulder at the ball, keep his head down, and hit the ball hard to the opposite field on a line or on the ground. Pop-ups are not accepted.

**Step 3** involves getting into the **spin hit** position. The hitter starts from his normal stance. When you call "spin," the hitter takes his normal stride, a 45-degree angle toward home plate, and stops. At this point his hands have not committed. All he has done is take his inward turn and stride; then you feed him the ball. All the hitter needs to do is keep the front shoulder closed and hit the ball hard to the opposite field on a line or on the ground and roll up on the back foot. What has been added is rolling the back foot, as well as placing the hitter much closer to what will eventually be his normal swing. But here again be sure to emphasize that the front shoulder stays in and closed and the head stays down on the ball.

**Step 4** in the overload drill involves no stopping. The hitter takes a full, 100-percent swing—a complete effort—except that he hits the ball to the opposite field on a line or on the ground. Once again, emphasize keeping the front shoulder in and the head down.

## DRILL #8
## *Spin Hit*
### (age 8 and older)

The **spin hit drill** has many applications. It can be used quite effectively for hitters:

- who overstride,
- who have a tendency to step away from the pitch into the bucket,
- who tend to lunge at the pitch,
- who have a problem hitting the ball to the opposite field,
- who make poor use of the back foot and hips, or
- who drop the hands.

In an identical manner to step 3 of the overload drill, call out "spin" as you are about to pitch (see Figure 8a).

Once he hears "spin," the hitter takes a short stride, about 4 inches, at a 45-degree angle toward the plate, steps on the big toe, and "lands on thin ice" (see Figures 8b and 8c). Then feed him the ball. All the hitter needs to do at this point is worry about hitting the ball hard, rolling up on the back foot, and thrusting the hips—that is, squishing the bug (see Figures 8c and 8d).

Keep in mind that merely pointing out that the hitter is overstriding does not get at the root of the problem. Inappropriate corrective measures, such as putting a bat in front of or behind the hitter when he steps in the bucket (strides away), will not help either. Hitters overstride because they have never learned how to balance themselves in any other way. They step away from the plate primarily because they are afraid of the ball, are too close to the plate, or have just developed a bad habit. Hitters lunge at pitches because they do not get an inward turn, they have found that lunge to be comfortable, or they are just being overly aggressive.

The spin-hit drill allows hitters to eliminate many things that can go wrong with their strokes and to work on feeling balanced and comfortable when they swing. If, at the beginning, a young hitter is taught a balanced and comfortable stride, he can correct stride mistakes easily if any should arise. Usually they are discovered by a coach. But if the hitter never learns to physically balance himself with a shorter stride, such a stride is not going to be attained.

The spin hit is a good example of a drill that can provide great benefits with very little effort. If the problem is not too severe, the drill should be executed briefly on a daily basis or even just twice a week. It does not require many swings—maybe five cuts in all. If the problem is severe, however, then the drill should be done every time that particular hitter takes batting practice.

You can maximize the results from the spin-hit drill if you use a short screen or an L-screen. (One is shown in Figure 11 on p. 94.) Pull the L-screen to within 20 or 30 feet of the hitter. Then get on one knee and feed the hitter strikes, giving him an opportunity to become comfortable with a new shorter stride. Be sure to position yourself behind the screen to avoid being hit.

**FIGURE 8**
*#8: The spin-hit drill.*

*A. The hitter waits to hear "spin" from the coach.*

*B. After hearing "spin," the hitter takes a short stride, steps on the big toe, and lands on thin ice.*

*C. The hitter rolls up on the back foot, thrusts his hips, and begins swinging at the ball.*

*D. The hitter completes the swing.*

## DRILL #9
## *Game Time*
(age 13 and older)

The ***game-time drill*** works well as a reward for hitters who have mastered the fundamentals of hitting or are moving in that direction. It gives a break in normal practice routines and allows the coach to work on game situations. This drill works best one-on-one, with the coach as the pitcher and the judge of balls, strikes, and hits. A variety of pitches should be thrown: If you can, throw curveballs; if not, throw fastballs mixed with change-ups. Pitches should be in and out, up and down, allowing the hitters to perform in different game situations.

If you cannot throw strikes, a pitching machine can serve as a good substitute, but be sure that the hitters get a variety of pitches. They can achieve variety by shifting position, moving up and back and in and out. Avoid extended periods of time on the grooved pitches that a machine often provides.

Begin game time in the first inning with no one on base and no outs. Suppose that the first hitter in the first inning gets a hit. You may shout to the new hitter, who now has no outs

### For The Advanced Hitter.......................................

With a man on third and less than two outs, the advanced hitter has three options:

1. *Hit a ground ball between shortstop and second base.*
2. *Hit a ball up in the strike zone. (Just swing at the ball without trying to swing up.)*
3. *Swing at a pitch that can be hit to the opposite field.*

*For most hitters, the first pitch is usually the best pitch to hit because pitchers want to get ahead in the count.*

and a man on first, "hit and run." Force him to execute the hit and run. If he does, there are now men on first and third with no outs. What is the hitter's responsibility now with a man on third and less than two outs? It is to score the runner. How does he propose to do that? The goal of a young hitter is to get a good pitch early in the count. With that pitch, there are three different options. He can either get a base hit, hit a sacrifice fly, or, if the infield is back, hit a ground ball away from the third baseman and pitcher. The hitter should try to execute one of these three options.

As a coach, you will be moving the hitter constantly from one of these sit-

uations to another. Suppose that the situation is two outs and either a man on second or a man on third. The hitter needs to be disciplined in his choice of balls to hit. He should make sure that he gets a good pitch to hit and that he can hit it hard in order to maximize his chances of scoring the run.

Suppose that the situation is the seventh inning with no outs and a man on first. You could ask for a sacrifice bunt or, if the game is tied, you might ask the hitter to take the next pitch, or you might choose to have him protect the runner if he is stealing. You can do anything that you want with this drill: Its purpose is to teach baseball, while making the learning process fun and challenging for the hitter. This drill is an excellent way to take hitters who are really doing well one step beyond the physical aspect into the mental aspect of hitting. Many major league pitchers play this simulated game during their pregame batting practice.

## DRILL #10
## *Low Pitch*
## (age 13 and older)

Pitches that give the hitter difficulty in games should be drilled. It is also valuable for a hitter to think about what the opposition is teaching its pitchers. For example, in youth leagues and older groups, pitchers are often instructed to throw as many knee-high fastballs on the outside part of the plate as they possibly can. Yet a hitting coach rarely works on such pitches with his players. Or perhaps a hitter is having trouble with low pitches. Other than seeing an occasional low pitch in batting practice, however, he probably never has a chance to focus on that particular pitch.

The **low-pitch drill** can be done using a batting tee. If the tee is a two-part tee with a top part that slides down into the bottom portion of the tee, take the top part off and place the ball on the bottom portion.

First, set the tee off the outside part of the plate in order to practice hitting a pitch that is low and outside. Have the player hit a ball placed on the tee. The hitter should not stand up straight and compromise his bat angle in order to hit the ball. He needs to flex both knees slightly in order to go down and get the ball (see Figure 9a). If he does not, the bat angle will not be level and the result will probably be a complete miss or a pop-up (flare) to the opposite field. Often if he imagines hitting such an outside pitch on the ground to the opposite field, the player will actually hit a line drive.

Once the hitter completes his swing and follow-through, he should stop and kneel down, lightly touching his back knee to the ground (see Figure 9b). At this point, you should check the hitter's balance. If he takes the cut and is off balance so that he cannot touch his back knee to the ground, he was probably not in a good position to hit. This checkpoint is always the final part of the low-pitch drill.

**FIGURE 9**
**#10: The**
**low-pitch drill.**

**A. Flex both knees slightly.**

**B. Bring the back knee down to the ground after the follow-through.**

Second, set the tee on the middle of the plate in order to practice hitting a pitch that is low and across the middle of the plate. The hitter again flexes the knees, but now attempts to hit the ball up the middle.

Third, set the tee on the inside part of the plate in order to practice hitting a pitch that is low and inside. To hit such a pitch, the player should (1) keep his head down, (2) hit the inside part of the ball, and (3) hit a line drive.

The low-pitch drill is not strictly for hitters with a problem hitting low pitches, but it can be incorporated into a regular practice for a team or an individual player. For example, if the player is hitting daily off a tee, the low-pitch drill should be part of his routine. In fact, hitters should always

work on inside pitches, outside pitches, high pitches, and low pitches, making them a normal part of their daily ritual.

## DRILL #11
### *High Pitch*
### (age 13 and older)

The goal of the **high-pitch drill** is to work on pitches in the top of the strike zone. If you have a young player who is not tall, you might be able to carry out this drill simply by raising the top half of the tee. For the older players (generally age 14–18 and older), you may need to raise the tee by placing it on something like a small block of wood. This will elevate the tee 5 or 6 inches to get the ball in the top of the strike zone.

# *For The Advanced Hitter*.................................................................

An excellent way to practice hitting high pitches is called the tomahawk swing. The hitter:

1. *thinks of sitting to hit the ball, bending the knees just a bit more,*
2. *leads the swing with the knob of the bat,*
3. *pulls down so that the head of the bat is above the ball, and*
4. *completes the swing.*

The swing is like attacking the ball with a tomahawk as seen in the figure. Bill Russell, formerly of the Los Angeles Dodgers, used this swing quite successfully.

**The tomahawk swing at a high pitch.**

**A. Think of sitting to hit the ball, bending the knees just a bit more.**

**B. Lead the swing with the knob of the bat.**

**C. Pull down so that the head of the bat is above the ball.**

**D. Continue the swing.**

**E. Complete the swing.**

Have the player hit a ball placed on the tee. During this drill, the hitter should not even think about flexing the front knee. He should just take his normal stride and normal swing (see Figure 10). The keys to hitting the high pitch are:

1. swing slightly down through the ball ("slap the hands down"),

2. lead with the knob of the bat at the ball and pull the hands down and across, forcing the shortest route to the high pitch, and

3. hit the ball hard and on a line.

Above all, the hitter does not want to hit underneath the ball, missing the ball completely and hitting the tee. If that happens, it is a sure sign that he needs to emphasize the preceding key steps.

## DRILL #12
## *Mirror Drill*
### (age 8 and older)

The **mirror drill** is one of Dusty Baker's favorites. Using a full-length mirror, position the hitter either sideways facing the mirror or looking at the mirror as though it were the pitcher. The hitter then takes a look at his

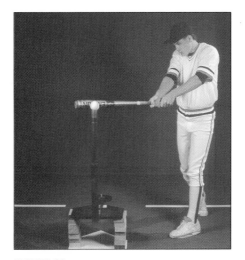

**FIGURE 10**
*#11: The high-pitch drill. Raise the tee to get the ball at the top of the strike zone.*

stance, stride, and inward turn and evaluates how he sets up and gets ready to hit. (If a shorter mirror must be used, the hitter can, of course, check himself from the waist up.) The goal of the drill is shadow hitting: If there is room, the hitter swings at an imaginary ball; if not, he can place pieces of tape on the mirror to represent balls in different locations.

In this drill, the hitter should make sure that his weight is evenly distributed and that his balance point is straight down through the center of the body. He should not lean either forward or too far back. At the same time, he can check many aspects of a

proper swing, such as the box, the head, eye angle (both eyes looking at the pitcher), front shoulder, hip, inward turn, and stride. Although it takes no more than a minute or two per day, the mirror drill is important in stressing key points to work on in improving the stroke. This drill can also be enhanced with the use of a video camera.

## DRILL #13
## *Short Screen*
### (age 6 and older)

The **short-screen drill** is one of Jeff Mercer's favorites. It gives the hitting instructor the opportunity to target pitches to specific locations with great accuracy.

Suppose you are throwing batting practice to your hitters from a distance of 50 to 60 feet. Most players will be lucky to hit the low outside target on the plate more than 4 or 5 times out of 10. If your goal were to practice low outside pitches, you would be wasting valuable practice time. If you know, however, that you can accurately throw 8 out of 10 pitches from that distance, pursue the drill in that manner.

To execute this drill satisfactorily, pull the short screen or L-screen to within 20 to 30 feet of the hitter. Get down on one knee, keeping as much of your body as you can behind the screen (see Figure 11), and throw pitches overhand to the hitter at the desired location. If he needs to work on low outside pitches, you have a much better chance of hitting that target since you are closer. High inside pitches can also be worked in an easy manner. If the hitter is successful with the inside pitch but weak with an outside pitch, feed about 80 percent of your pitches to the outside part of the plate. To maintain his confidence and enthusiasm, however, spend the remaining 20 percent of the time feeding him those pitches that he hits most successfully.

The short-screen drill accomplishes two goals:

1. It allows the hitter to get a lot of extra cuts that he normally could not get from regulation distance.
2. It maximizes the hitter's practice efforts.

This drill also relieves many frustrations of youth league coaches who have trouble throwing strikes. When

20–30 feet

**FIGURE 11**
*#13: The short-screen drill. Pitching from behind a short screen allows the coach to throw pitches to a specific area with greater consistency.*

there is a lack of control in pitching batting practice, two problems occur:

1. Because the hitter is constantly swinging at pitches out of the strike zone, he cannot work effectively.
2. The hitter spends most of his time trying to get out of the way of the pitch to avoid being hurt.

Thus the efforts of both the coach and the hitter are maximized by using the short-screen drill.

Hitters need to develop quick hands. Certainly strengthening the hands using hand grips, half rubber balls, or

YOU CAN TEACH HITTING

wrist exercises will help. Another method involves isolating the hands, that is, overloading them to a degree and forcing them to work. This method is a modification of the short-screen drill. Set the short screen up within 20 to 30 feet of the hitter. Then throw practice pitches to the hitter either over the middle of the plate or on the inside half. The hitter should work on throwing the hands as quickly as he can, while still pulling the bat through. The better the hitter executes the drill, the harder you should throw, in order to isolate the hands even more. Remind the hitter that he should still let the hips lead the way in carrying out this drill.

# DRILL #14
## *Now Drill*
## (age 13 and older)

The **now drill** is effective for hitters who have difficulty waiting for pitches and, as a result, have trouble hitting the ball to the opposite field because they simply don't know how. Typically, this problem occurs because the hitter does not understand where the ball should be when he begins his swing. It seems simple to tell the hitter to wait and let the ball get to him be-

fore he swings. Unfortunately, this is easier said by coaches than done by hitters.

In this drill, you will be pitching from regulation distance. Tell the hitter not to swing for several pitches. He should instead visualize hitting a ball hard to the opposite field. This visualization will prepare him mentally to handle a ball to the opposite field and to teach him physically where the ball is when his swing begins. When the ball gets so close that the hitter thinks he can't wait any longer to execute the swing and hit the ball to the opposite field, he says "now" instead of swinging. He should do this whenever he feels the time is right, whether the ball is 3 feet or maybe 10 feet in front of home plate.

After practicing several "now" pitches, the hitter will begin to get a feel for the location of the ball. Then have him swing and hit the ball to the opposite field. Almost without fail the hitter will do so with much greater ease than he did before going through the drill.

It's amazing to both hitters and to those who watch this drill just how close the ball is to the hitter on an outside pitch before he must begin his stroke. Most hitters "hook" an outside pitch—that is, they open the front shoulder prematurely and the bat head actually hooks the outside of the ball. Right-handers tend to ground out to the shortstop and lefthanders tend to ground out to second base. A delay of just a split second in the swing might result in a double to right or left center field.

What the hitter discovers through the now drill is that on an outside pitch, he should wait until the ball is approximately 4 to 8 inches in front of the plate. At that point he releases his hips, "squishes the bug," and drives his hips and hands toward the ball. Up until that point, however, he has not moved forward into the swing. On an inside pitch, the ball will be somewhere in the vicinity of 2 to 3 feet in front of the plate before the hitter actually begins to swing. The hitter will find in executing this drill that there is quite a difference between the spot for swinging at an outside pitch and the spot for an inside pitch (see Figure 12).

Although the swing itself is exactly the same for both an outside and an inside pitch, the player must hesitate for a split second before hitting an

outside pitch. Physically demonstrating where the ball should be when he starts his swing will provide him with a better feel for the timing of the swing. During the drill, ask the player, "Where was the ball when you said 'now'?" Most often they will point either over the plate or slightly in front

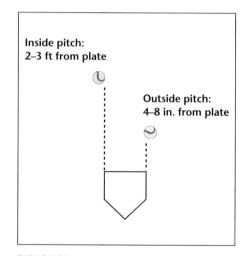

**FIGURE 12**
*#14: Location of pitches for the now drill.*

of it. Your response is then, "Would you believe that it's 4 to 8 inches in front of the plate? Isn't it amazing that you can wait that long to swing and still be quick enough to execute the swing?"

YOU CAN TEACH HITTING

# DRILL #15
## *1-2-3 Drill*
### (age 8 and older)

The ***1-2-3 drill*** is excellent to use with young hitters to begin development of proper batting habits. It is also a good corrective drill for hitters who have difficulty in executing the proper techniques of the swing. It helps to have a parent or coach with the hitter when he is executing the 1-2-3 drill so that the hitter can be prevented from rushing through the drill and specific problems can be diagnosed.

Using the tee (see Figure 13), the hitter executes the drill as follows:

1. He assumes the proper stance,
2. takes his inward turn and stride, and
3. rolls up on the back foot and thrusts the hips ("squishes the bug") and swings.

In this manner, he begins developing the position of his back foot in the normal batting stroke. Continual work at this drill also assists the hitter in forming a good stride habit, a short stride, and, in the case of a young hit-

**A. Assume the proper stance.**

**B. Take the inward turn and stride.**

ter, a 45-degree angle toward home plate.

Of course, it is always better to isolate a hitter's specific problems and have him do repetitive, corrective drills rather than just swing the bat. Working off a tee on a 1-2-3 drill for 5 minutes is much more effective than swinging incorrectly at live pitching for half an hour. It is important to isolate the hitter's problems and correct them through a repetitive, methodical approach. Then the hitter can take his live cuts and develop a well-rounded swing. The 1-2-3 drill is a good start toward developing that swing.

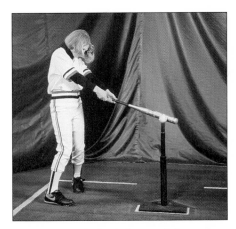

**C. Roll up on the back foot and thrust the hips ("squish the bug") and swing.**

**FIGURE 13**
**#15: The 1-2-3 drill.**

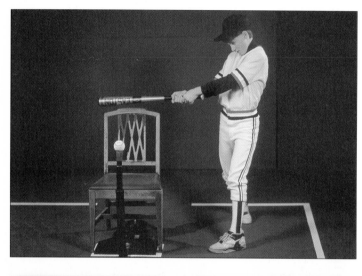

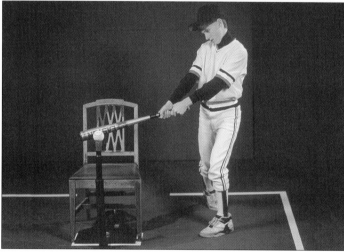

**FIGURE 14**
*#16: The chair drill.*

## DRILL #16
### *Chair Drill*
(age 13 and older)

The **chair drill** is an excellent drill for the hitter who tends to uppercut. Place a tee on the inside half of the plate and an old metal or wood folding chair behind the tee with the seat closest to the tee (see Figure 14). To execute this drill properly, the hitter must swing with a *slightly downward* angle. The tee is best placed just slightly lower than the back of the chair so that the hitter must physically swing slightly down through the ball. If he does not, he will uppercut the ball, hit the chair before ever reaching the ball, and get a loud warning that he has not executed the drill properly.

There is little benefit to turning the chair around the opposite way and forcing the hitter to swing almost completely straight down through the ball. It is much better to have the seat face the tee, making the hitter take a slightly downward plane with his swing. The possibility of hitting the chair forces the player to concentrate on correcting his bat angle.

This drill can be done a couple of times a week. If you are frequently using the tee or if the hitter has a particularly severe problem, use it more often, say, every day. It is an excellent drill for teaching the hitter what type of stroke he needs in order to successfully hit line drives and ground balls.

## DRILL #17
## *Hip Thrust*
## (age 10 and older)

The **hip-thrust drill** is useful for the hitter who has difficulty in rolling up on the back foot and thrusting the hips ("squishing the bug"). It is our opinion that hitters need more practice on this drill than *any* other. When a hitter does not utilize his hips effectively, he is not using the strongest half of his body. This makes it difficult for him to hit either an outside pitch or an inside pitch into fair territory.

In this drill, the hitter rests the bat on or slightly off his shoulder. When the ball gets close to the plate, he visualizes hitting either to the opposite field or to the pull or power field. Then, instead of swinging, he rotates his hips

**FIGURE 15**
*#17: The hip-thrust drill.*

and calls out "thrust." Thus, as the ball gets close, the hitter rolls up on his back foot and thrusts his hips through the ball. He does not swing at the ball—he just "squishes the bug," getting his body in a position to help the hands drive the bat through the contact zone (see Figure 15).

Just 3–5 repetitions daily of the hip-thrust drill works well. To vary the drill, have the hitter take 3 or 4 hip thrusts as if hitting to the opposite field, then 3 or 4 hip thrusts to the pull field, and then let him start swinging.

For hitters who have difficulty utilizing the hips, this practice drill is critical in acquiring skill at hitting.

## DRILL #18
## *Iso Bat*
## (age 6 and older)

The **iso-bat drill** is good for young hitters who are not yet into lifting weights, because it maximizes the strength of the hitter's swing without weight machines or barbells. *Iso* comes from the word *isometric,* which means "tension gathering."

**FIGURE 16**
*#18: The iso-bat drill.*

*A. The beginning: resisting the swing.*

*B. Halfway through the iso-bat drill.*

*C. The end of the iso-bat drill.*

Sound hitting fundamentals are to be followed. Thus the hitter is to roll up on the back foot, thrust the hips, keep the head down with his chin on the chest, extend the arms completely in a straight line from the front arm right on down through the bat, and slowly swing the bat. The goal is to get the hitter to the point where he extends the arms with the bat out over the plate with his head down as though he were going to hit a ball up the middle. Then place your hand in front of the bat and slightly resist the player very lightly all the way around to the follow-through position as he finishes his swing (see Figure 16). This develops strength in the hitter's swing. The resistance should not be so heavy as to force the hitter to change any portion of his stroke just to be able to follow through.

The younger hitter should do 5–10 repetitions per day, while the older hitter who enjoys doing this drill and sees some merit in it would benefit from 10–20 repetitions per day. This drill can also be easily done at home with a parent.

There is a variation of this drill for older hitters who have more strength. With a rope, hang a small tire from a tree limb or post. The hitter then takes an old bat and hits the tire. The tire will rotate and provide a fair amount of resistance. Be sure that once the hitter has made contact with the tire, he drives through it and completes the follow-through. He should not stop as soon as he makes contact with the tire. The drill is of no value if the hitter does not get a good follow-through.

# DRILL #19
## *Counts and Situations*
(age 13 and older)

The **counts-and-situations** drill is similar to the game-time drill in that it constantly changes the pattern of thought for the hitter. In fact, in the counts-and-situations drill, the tasks change much more rapidly than in the game-time drill. Using either a pitching machine or live pitches, start with an 0–0 count. Then go to a 1–0 count, to a 2–0, to a 3–1, to a 3–0, and then to an 0–2. Skip around constantly, putting hitters into different counts that force them to rapidly deal with situations that can occur during a game.

As a further example, you might start with a 2–0 count, no one on, and no outs. What must the hitter do? He should be looking for a fastball and limiting his swinging zone a bit—that is, he will not swing at a pitch unless he likes it. If the pitch is slightly out of the swinging zone and is a strike, but the hitter does not like it, he should let it go. He will still be ahead 2–1.

You might then switch the hitter to an 0–2 count, with no one on and no outs. In this case, the hitter should protect the plate regardless of what pitch comes in. When the pitch is close to the strike zone, he must take a swing. Then you might switch to an 0–0 count, with a man on third and no outs.

You can also vary the drill by eliminating the counts and just making use of the situations. For example, call out "hit and run," "sacrifice bunt," "man on third with no outs, and score the runner." Or try "hit a sacrifice fly" or "hit the ball on the ground to move the runner over."

This drill constantly challenges the hitter mentally to execute the tasks at hand. At the same time, it helps him develop a sense of confidence about each situation as he approaches the plate. The situations will become ingrained in his mind because he will have been through them so many times.

## DRILL #20
### *Up and Down*
(age 15 and older)

Not to be confused with the high-pitch or low-pitch drills, the **up-and-down drill** teaches hitters how to hit balls in the air and on the ground without changing their stroke. If the hitter's goal is to hit a ground ball, what part of the ball must he hit? The answer is the top half of the ball. If he wants to hit a flyball, what part must he hit? The answer is the bottom half. The point of this drill is to teach the hitter that he must change his *target,* not his stance or stroke. Instead of looking at the middle of the ball and trying to hit it, the hitter now tries to hit either the top or the bottom half (see Figure 17).

Without practice, a hitter cannot go to the plate and execute this skill to perfection. An advanced hitter, however, who has already achieved good fundamentals and has been through the other drills, can acquire this skill, which certainly gives him and his team an advantage at the plate.

Many hitters who perform well with no one on base tend to press once a

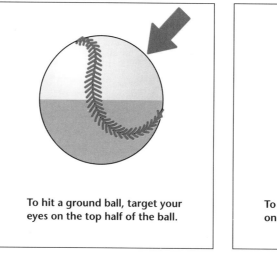

To hit a ground ball, target your eyes on the top half of the ball.

**A.**

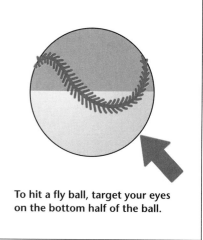

To hit a fly ball, target your eyes on the bottom half of the ball.

**B.**

**FIGURE 17**
*#20: The up-and-down drill.*

runner is in scoring position. Such a hitter has not practiced or even thought about how to accomplish the task at hand. He only knows that he is supposed to get the ball in the air to the outfield, but in attempting to do so, he changes his stroke. This generally results in his uppercutting the ball and either missing completely or hitting a pop-up to the infield. This drill will help him learn to target the appropriate part of the ball rather than change his stroke.

We close this chapter with a summary

table covering what has been discussed in Chapters 3 and 4. The 10 most common hitting mistakes are listed along with the 20 drills considered in this chapter. An × indicates that the drill in that row can be used to correct the mistake listed in the column above. Drills without × marks are specialty drills that do not pertain to correcting a particular mistake.

Remember that you may not need all 20 drills for all your players and that you should individualize the drills to the needs of each player.

# Hitting Drills

## Ten Most Common Hitting Mistakes

| Drill | Stance and Stride | Grip | Box | Dead Stop Hitter | Back Foot Lockout | Bat Angle | Front Shoulder Early Release/ Quick Hip | Follow-Through | Tracking and Head Position | Fear of the Ball |
|---|---|---|---|---|---|---|---|---|---|---|
| #1 Fence | | | × | | | × | × | × | | |
| #2 One-Hand | | × | | | | | | × | | |
| #3 Right/Left/Middle | | | | | | | | | × | |
| #4 1-2-3-4 | | | | × | | | | | | |
| #5 Soft-Toss Breaker* | | | | | | | | | | |
| #6 Bat Behind the Back | | | | | × | | | | | |
| #7 Overload | | | | | | | × | | | |
| #8 Spin Hit | × | | × | | × | × | × | × | | |
| #9 Game Time* | | | | | | | | | | |
| #10 Low Pitch* | | | | | | | | | | |
| #11 High Pitch* | | | | | | | | | | |
| #12 Mirror Drill | × | × | × | × | × | × | × | × | × | |
| #13 Short Screen | × | | × | × | | × | | × | | |
| #14 Now Drill | | | | | | | × | | | |
| #15 1-2-3 | × | | | | × | | × | | | |
| #16 Chair Drill | | | | | | × | | | | |
| #17 Hip Thrust | | | | | × | | | | | |
| #18 Iso Bat* | | | | | | | | | | |
| #19 Counts and Situations* | | | | | | | | | | |
| #20 Up and Down* | | | | | | | | | | |

*Specialty drill.

# CHAPTER FIVE

# Offensive Weapons

The Sacrifice Bunt

Bunting for a Base Hit

The Hit and Run

The Bunt and Run

The Squeeze Bunt

**Marv.** *Through my years coaching 12-year-olds, players have come to me with very little ability to bunt. The next time I coach, I'd like to spend much more time on bunting. I think it would be a fascinating experiment to have every hitter bunt for an entire inning. What do you think?*

**Dusty.** You might make a lot of people angry, but it would certainly make a point.

**Jeff.** *My father was my Little League coach. His favorite baseball story is about the first time we played a particular team who literally wiped us off the diamond. The coach and the players were so arrogant and outspoken that it really disturbed my dad. He couldn't wait until we played them again.*

*The second time, in our first at bat, we managed to get the first three runners on base. My dad had our fourth hitter, the strongest batter on the team, lay down a bunt. The other team was caught so off-guard that it made three bad overthrows. By the time the dust had settled, three runs were scored and our fourth hitter was on third base. The tactic took the wind right out of our opponent's sails. We went on to win the game 20–5. The bunt turned out to be a powerful offensive weapon!*

In this chapter, we cover five important offensive weapons: the

1. sacrifice bunt,
2. bunt for a hit,
3. hit and run,
4. bunt and run, and
5. squeeze bunt.

Note that four of these weapons involve the bunt—the act of hitting a short ground ball somewhere in a band consisting of a circular sector between the pitcher and the catcher. In general, bunting is an overlooked weapon in baseball today, especially with younger teams. One reason is simply that the bunt is not a very glamorous task to perform. Another reason is the more frequent use of the designated hitter (the DH), who usually replaces the pitcher, the weakest hitter in the batting order at the major league level. Formerly, if a pitcher came to bat with a runner on base, he was asked to advance the runner with a bunt. With the designated hitter, the pitcher rarely comes to the plate, so the bunt is used less often. The main reason, however, is that the bunt is difficult both to teach and to learn.

# The Sacrifice Bunt

Using the **sacrifice bunt**, the hitter deliberately gives himself up as an out in order to advance base runners to positions from which they can score most easily. The goal of the hitter is to move the runner from either first to second or second to third, or both, if there are two runners on base at the same time.

There are three methods of sacrifice bunting:

1. squaring around,
2. pivoting around, and
3. the offset method.

Although the first two are frequently used, we do not recommend them for young hitters. However, we do recommend the third method for hitters at *all* age levels.

When **squaring around**, the hitter moves his back foot forward to a position parallel with his front foot (See Figure 1a on the following page.). This method of bunting often renders the hitter susceptible to being hit by a pitch.

When **pivoting around**, the hitter simply swivels on his feet and opens his upper body to the point at which he can bunt the ball (see Figure 1b). Compared to the third type of bunt, this method decreases the chances of the bunt being fair.

The preferred way to bunt, called the **offset method**, gives the hitter a better opportunity to put the ball in play and execute the sacrifice bunt. Just before the pitcher gets to his balance point (or shows the hitter his hip pocket), the hitter begins shifting around, but in a manner slightly different than that shown in Figures 1(a) and (b). As he begins to turn to face the pitcher, he almost physically throws the bat at the pitcher. In other words, he directs the bat head at the pitcher. Such a motion brings his back foot up and out slightly in front of the plate. For a right-handed batter, this method will put his right foot slightly in front of his left foot (see Figures 1c and d). For a left-handed batter, the opposite occurs—that is, his left foot will be slightly in front of his right foot (see Figure 1e). This puts the hitter at an angle out over the plate, maximizing his chances of laying down the bunt in fair territory. Be sure to caution the hitter to stay inside the batter's box.

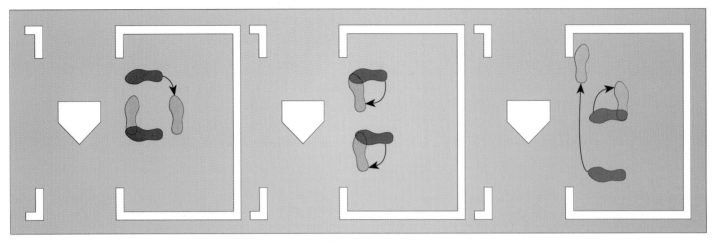

**A. Squaring around.**

**B. Pivoting around.**

**C. The offset method.**

**FIGURE 1**
*Methods of bunting.*

**D. The offset method for a right-handed hitter.**

**E. The offset method for a left-handed hitter.**

YOU CAN TEACH HITTING

The thumbs-up sign —  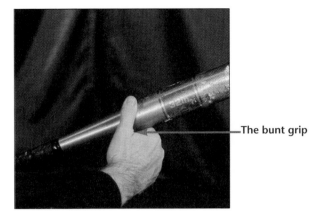 —The bunt grip

**FIGURE 2**
*The bunt grip.*

*A. The hand in the "thumbs up" position about to grip the bat.*

*B. The bunt grip.*

Once the bunter gets his back foot out in front of the plate, he places his hands and the bat at the top of the strike zone. At that point, any pitch that comes in above the bat will be a ball, and he simply pulls back. He must be sure to bunt only strikes. Since the hitter will generally not be in the position of having to bunt the pitch, if he draws a walk, so much the better.

When the hitter has the bat at the top of the strike zone, he bends his knees slightly, keeping his elbows in—neither one should be flared out. The elbows act as shock absorbers. When the ball makes contact with the bat, they should give slightly. Ask the hitter to imagine that there is a fielder's glove on the end of the bat and that he is going to catch the ball in that glove. Another way to think of the

contact between bat and ball is to contrast it with normal hitting. In normal hitting, the player hits the ball with the bat, whereas when bunting, he lets the ball hit the bat.

To teach the grip on a bunt, have the hitter show you the "thumbs up" sign with his top hand. Then place the bat, tilted up, right in the wedge formed by the top of his forefingers and thumb (see Figure 2). The hitter should be careful to keep from wrapping his fingers around the bat. If he does so, part of the fingers would face the ball, setting up the possibility of smashing or breaking a finger. The hand should be positioned at a point on the bat that enables the hitter to balance the bat as though it were held exactly level. For most hitters, this point is an inch or two below the label.

# For The Advanced Hitter.....................

*Pitchers are often taught to throw the ball high in the strike zone when a hitter is attempting a sacrifice bunt. If the pitcher loses control and the pitch comes at the batter, especially at a fast speed, it may be easier for the hitter to avoid the pitch if he is pivoting around to bunt rather than using the offset method.*

As it makes contact, the force of the ball knocks the bat back slightly into the hitter's hand, which absorbs the force of the ball and kills its momentum. The object is not to bunt the ball hard, sending it directly back to the pitcher or the first or third baseman. This would cause the lead runner to be thrown out quickly or trapped in a rundown. Should the hitter desire to hit the ball farther, say, in a "push bunt," he simply holds the top hand more firmly on the bat, not allowing the bat to be knocked back in his hand. Usually the goal is to have the ball hit the bat above the top hand about halfway between there and the end of the bat—near the "sweet spot."*

*The term "sweet spot" is discussed in Chapter 9.

You can explore the benefits of the offset method for the young hitter as follows. Have the bunter square around with his feet parallel. Then see how far back into the strike zone he can track the pitch while still successfully laying down the bunt (even though, for now, it might land in foul territory). Then have him try to bunt with his back foot out in front of the plate. Generally, the hitter will notice that he can't track the ball back into the strike zone nearly as far. The offset method gives the batter a much better angle and thus a better chance of successfully putting the bunt in play.

One of the keys to successful bunting is to *keep the bat tilted up*. The barrel of the bat should be tilted up much more so than the knob of the bat (see Figures 1 and 2). A flat angle is conducive not only to popping the ball straight up but also to running the risk of turning a potential sacrifice into a double play. By angling the barrel of the bat up, the hitter will rarely pop the ball straight up. A foul pop-up will shoot off to the left or right, making it more difficult for the catcher or the first or third baseman to run it down. The hitter usually fails at bunting when he either levels out the bat, pokes at the ball, or goes out after it.

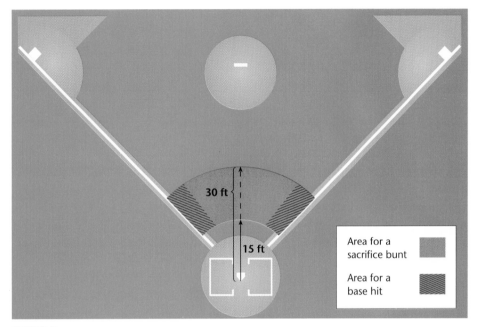

30 ft

15 ft

Area for a
sacrifice bunt

Area for a
base hit

**FIGURE 3**
*Ideal bunt locations.*

Simple as it sounds, another key to bunting is to remember to bunt the ball first and *then* run. Many hitters start running and then try to bunt the ball.

The ideal location for a sacrifice bunt is anywhere in a circular band between 15 to 30 feet out from the plate and 1 foot out from the foul lines and in fair territory on the first- and third-base lines (see Figure 3).

In general, it is easier for a left-hander to bunt to the third-base side and a right-hander to bunt to the first-base side. Where to place a bunt depends, however, on the game situation or the particular bunt defense. For example, if the first baseman is moving in toward the plate to defend against the bunt of a right-handed hitter, it would help if the hitter is able to bunt down the third-base line in order to avoid losing the lead runner. In all cases, though, the hitter's goal is to keep the ball out of the air.

We cannot overemphasize that if you don't ask your players to bunt the ball on a daily basis, it's *extremely difficult* to expect them to execute the bunt in a game. Bunting is not easy. In fact, it is often a traumatic experience for younger players, who generally find it uncomfortable to have their hands that close to the ball. If you want to use the bunt in a game, you must continually practice it beforehand.

## Bunting for a Base Hit

When **bunting for a base hit**, the hitter should try to place the ball 12 to 18 inches from the edge of the grass along the foul line and within a band 15 to 30 feet from the plate (see Figure 3). A ball that rolls on the dirt portion of the baseline has a greater chance of going foul.

It is important that the hitter know *when* to shift into position to bunt for a base hit since it differs from the timing for the sacrifice bunt. When attempting to bunt for a base hit, the hitter doesn't want to shift too soon and tip off the fact that he's going to

bunt before the pitcher has reached the release point of the pitch. If he does, the defenders will, of course, charge the ball sooner and lessen the chances of getting a base hit. The hitter should not shift until the pitcher's arm is up in the "L" position, ready to throw.

Bunting for a base hit is different for a left-handed batter than for a right-handed batter. The left-handed batter uses the offset method (see Figure 1e). He brings his back foot straight out toward the pitcher, not toward the first-base line, and stays in the box until he is sure that he has laid down the bunt successfully. Once done, he steps with his right foot and runs to first base as fast as he can. Many left-handers incorrectly pick up the left foot and bring it out almost around to the first-base line, thus running to first before they get the ball down.

As we mentioned earlier, it's typically easier for the left-handed hitter to bunt down the third-base line. It also forces the third baseman into a tough play because he has a long throw to first base. There is some advantage, however, for a left-hander who has a lot of speed to "drag bunt" the ball down the first-base line. The term "drag bunt" means that the batter begins moving out of the box as he bunts, with the bat dragging along behind. The batter almost drops the bat toward the ball as he leaves the box.

Bunting for a base hit is simpler for a right-handed batter. The hitter drops his right foot straight back from his normal stance position, gets the bat head out in front of the plate, with the bat angled up, and lays down the ball. The first step out of the box is with the right foot (see Figure 4), which points to the first-base bag as though the hitter were running straight to first base.

Any hitter can pick up some percentage points on his batting average and be an asset to his team by knowing how to bunt the ball properly. If he doesn't bunt the ball into fair territory, however, being the fastest runner alive will be of no value. The hitter must first execute the bunt properly: holding the bat at the top of the strike zone, with the bat head angled up and the elbows used as shock absorbers, catching the ball on the bat, and bunting the ball into fair territory. Then *after bunting properly*, he gets out of the box as quickly as possible.

The decision to bunt for a base hit is

**FIGURE 4**
*A right-handed hitter bunting for a base hit.*

most often left up to the hitter. Even a power hitter with very little speed can pick up 4 to 6 bunt hits per year merely by catching the opposition off guard. Power hitters in the lineup generally find infielders playing exceptionally deep. An unsuspecting third baseman will not be looking for a bunt. In the right situation, the strong hitter can be as great an asset to his team by bunting his way on base as by hitting the long ball.

Bunts, both sacrifice and for base hits, create opportunities to score. A difficult situation is created for the defense when they are forced to react hurried-

## For The Advanced Hitter.......................................

The advanced right-handed hitter can bunt for a base hit as follows. As the bat is moved to meet the ball, the hitter takes a slight step toward home plate with the back foot moving toward first base, being careful at the same time not to step out of the batter's box. This allows for a quicker run to first base.

'Dropping the back foot, as was recommended for the young hitter, tips off the third baseman. Because the hitter's weight is back, it slows his momentum in running to first base. In order to drop the back foot, young hitters also have a tendency to step out of the batter's box.

ly to cover a bunt. Fielders don't have much time to execute the bunt defense in a game. Actually, most teams at the amateur level don't practice bunt defense because they don't often see opposing teams bunting. Frequently, an attempted sacrifice bunt leads to an overthrow, allowing a runner to move from first to third base with the bunter ending up on second base. This clearly places the offense in a great situation and puts additional pressure on the defense.

Bunting can be an effective tactic. Not only can it help the team win, it can also help a hitter bounce out of a minor unfortunate period, or slump.

## The Hit and Run

The **hit and run** is the only offensive weapon considered here that does not involve the bunt. Its primary objectives are to advance a runner at least two bases by opening up a hole in the defense and to get the hitter on base.

Typically, in the hit-and-run situation, there is a runner on first base who appears to be stealing second. Actually, he waits a split second longer than he would in a normal steal to avoid being picked off and negating the hit and run. Since there is a runner moving from first to second, some defender has to cover second base. Generally, a right-handed batter will pull the ball to the left side toward the shortstop or third baseman. Thus the shortstop stays in position and the second baseman covers second base.

As the runner progresses halfway to second base, he looks over his left shoulder to see whether the ball has been hit and, if so, where. The hitter must swing at *any* pitch, because any ball that the catcher can react to, catch, and throw increases the risk of having the base runner thrown out at second. The object is for the hitter to protect the runner both by swinging at the ball and by hitting it through the hole that the second baseman vacates in order to cover second base. That hole is somewhere between the second-base bag and the position of the first baseman. The goal is to hit the ball past the infielders into the outfield. The batter gets a base hit, and the runner is usually able to continue to third base.

To execute an effective hit and run, the batter *must* hit the ball on the ground. If he hits it in the air, where it can be caught, the runner on first base will probably end up on second in the nearly impossible position of trying to get back to first to prevent the double play.

The hit and run is not often used with a left-handed hitter, but the tactic can still be effective. In that case, the shortstop covers second base and the second baseman stays in position. The goal of the left-hander is to hit the ball through the hole left by the shortstop. The only disadvantage is that the runner on first base, who is now attempting to go to third, often finds the ball in front of him in left field, with the leftfielder having only a short throw to third base. Properly executed, though, the left-handed hit and run can provide the desired results: runners on first and third and no additional outs.

## The Bunt and Run

The **bunt and run** is designed primarily to advance a base runner. The procedure is quite similar to the hit and run, except the hitter bunts rather than swings at the ball. It is used typically with a runner on first base and

less than two outs. The bunt and run can frequently accomplish one goal of the hit and run: advancing the runner from first to third base. Sometimes it can accomplish the other result: getting a base hit for the batter.

If a left-handed hitter is at the plate and the defense is playing standard coverages, the instant the base runner takes off to steal second base, the shortstop covers second. In this case, it is more effective to bunt down the third-base line, because this forces the third baseman to field the ball. The shortstop, having moved with the pitch to cover second, is not in any position to cover third. Thus third base is unprotected and the third-base coach can judge whether or not to bring the runner on to third. The bunt and run is thus more appropriate for a left-handed hitter since his natural inclination is to bunt down the third-base line. In many situations, the confusion created by the bunt and run allows both the hitter to beat the bunt out and a slow runner to advance one base or more.

Suppose that there is a right-handed hitter at the plate when the bunt and run is called. Suppose further that the second baseman is going to cover sec-

## For The Advanced Hitter.................................

*There are various defensive strategies that can be used in a bunt situation. The more advanced hitter may be able to adjust how he bunts depending on the defense. Suppose there are runners on first and second and he anticipates that the shortstop will cover third. In that case, he might bunt down the first-base line.*

ond base, letting both the shortstop and third baseman stay in position to assist on the third-base side. In this case, there are two choices: to bunt either toward third base or down the first-base line. It is generally easier for a right-handed hitter to press the right side and force the first baseman to make a long throw to third. However, if the hitter is adept enough at bunting, the bunt down the third-base line can create some confusion for the defense, particularly if the third baseman must field the ball. If the shortstop is caught napping, the offense is in a good position to bring the runner all the way over to third base. The goal is to place as much pressure on the defense as possible. Generally, an ill-prepared defense will crack and make the desired mistake.

In the final analysis, the decision whether or not to try a bunt and run really depends on the ability of the hitter. If he is a left-handed hitter, can he drop a bunt down the third-base line? This is the easiest bunt for most left-handers. If he is a right-handed hitter, can he bunt only down the first-base line, or is he equally proficient at bunting down the third-base line? If he can do the latter, then he probably should.

## The Squeeze Bunt

Another important offensive weapon is the **squeeze bunt**, which is used primarily to score a runner from third in the later stages of the game either

to tie the game or go ahead. The key to the squeeze bunt is that the base runner on third must time his break exactly—that is, when the pitcher is at the point in his delivery when he cannot change the direction of his pitch to some other part of the plate. If the base runner is too early, the pitcher can change direction and throw the ball high or even at the hitter, making it very difficult for the hitter to execute the bunt. Thus the base runner from third must break when the pitcher has the ball at the point of release. The hitter also waits as long as possible, making sure that he can both execute the bunt and protect the runner. It's absolutely essential as well that the hitter lay the bunt down in fair territory so that the runner can score from third base.

A note of caution regarding the squeeze bunt. It is critical that both the runner and especially the batter comprehend the sign for the squeeze bunt. If the hitter misses the sign and swings away, pulling the ball toward him down the third-base line, the runner can be in danger. A way to avoid this is for the third-base coach to give the sign. Then the hitter signals back to both the runner and the coach that he has the sign.

# Offensive Weapons

- **Sacrifice Bunt**: Use the offset method for younger hitters. Bring the back foot up toward the pitcher and tilt the bat up. Locate the ball in a band 15 to 30 feet from the catcher.

- **Bunt for a Base Hit**: Use the offset method for a left-handed batter. For a right-handed batter, move the right foot back. Locate the ball 15 to 30 feet from the catcher and 12 to 18 inches from the edge of the grass along either foul line.

- **Hit and Run**: The runner starts to run, the infielder covers second, and the ball is hit into the open hole.

- **Bunt and Run**: Best done with a left-handed hitter. The runner on first starts to run and the ball is bunted down the third-base line. If third base is not covered, the runner moves there.

- **Squeeze Bunt**: The runner on third base breaks at the point when the pitcher cannot change the direction of the pitch. The ball is bunted in fair territory without popping up. The hitter waits to shift into bunt position until the ball is at the pitcher's release point.

# CHAPTER SIX

# Practice Organization for Teams

**Station Work**

**Situational Hitting**

**Enhancing Competition**

**Marv.** *I'm sure that many coaches affected your career. Can you tell us about two of your professional coaches and describe their assets?*

**Dusty.** Bill Lucas was the Farm Director and Assistant General Manager of the Atlanta Braves. At the time he was the highest ranking black executive not only in the Atlanta organization, but in all of baseball. He treated everybody equally without regard to color. He was tough, but fair. If he believed in you, he let you know it and was not afraid to stick his neck out for you.

Jim Gilliam, one of my coaches when I played for the Los Angeles Dodgers, really helped me refine my hitting skills and realize that baseball is a daily game. He was the first coach who forced us to play situational games during batting practice. Instead of normal batting practice, it was a game every time we got in the cage. This increased my concentration. Batting practice was fun, but serious business as well. How you practice is how you play. He was so in tune with us that he immediately knew when problems off the field were affecting a player's on-the-field performance.

A lthough all baseball players love to play the game, many do not enjoy practice at all. Organized practice, however, is an important aspect of running a baseball team. It is essential that practices be planned for the most effective use of time. Often coaches waste time in practice, frustrating both the players and their parents, who know their children have other obligations such as schoolwork. A crisply run, well-organized practice is one that players can look forward to and enjoy and parents will appreciate.

We split practice organization into two categories: station work and situational hitting. While consideration of age is made in some places, age differentiation is given more careful coverage in Chapter 7.

## Station Work

Station work can be done on a daily basis, though it is important to vary the work from time to time. Although we have stressed the importance of repetition when learning the fundamentals of hitting, the same practice routine can become boring. To avoid some of the boredom of repetitious practice, five different stations, or

**FIGURE 1**
*Hitting whiffle balls.*

components, might be included in a normal team practice. Described here is a team-based hitting practice. It does not include individual work with a specific player.

The *first* station—always a favorite—is the **whiffle-ball** station. The little whiffle golf balls used by golfers to warm up are the best for this work. Rather than being a solid ball, they have holes in them and do not travel very far. Thus there is little likelihood of injury if someone is hit. Use the whiffle balls with two or three players, that is, one hitting, one pitching, and the others, if any, fielding. This station allows the hitters to get many quality cuts in a short period of time.

The use of whiffle balls also allows a parent, who may not feel very proficient at baseball, to provide excellent hitting practice for his or her child (see Figure 1). It is quite easy to throw strikes. Rag balls, sock balls, and badminton birdies can also be used, and the drill can be done in a small area—say, a garage or a large family room. The important idea is that the hitter takes a lot of swings in a convenient, effective manner while looking at and following the ball. This drill is effective for hitters of all ages!

## For The Advanced Hitter.....................

*Do you think whiffle balls are for only small children and young hitters? In 1981, there was a major league baseball strike. During that strike period, Dusty Baker spent a lot of time practicing with whiffle balls. After the strike, he had the highest batting average in the National League!*

Whiffle ball practice also develops hand and eye coordination. No ball moves in quite the same fashion as a whiffle ball. But if a hitter trains himself to follow that little whiffle ball, the baseball will seem bigger, and therefore easier, to follow and hit.

The *second* component, or station, is **live hitting** on the actual baseball field.

The *third* station is **tee work**, either with a baseball or a tennis ball, possibly into a backstop. If a backstop is not available, try using a porta-sock, which is a freestanding net with a sock in the back, much like kickers use on the sideline of a football game. The hitter hits off the tee into a hole in the screen and the ball is caught in the sock netting.

The *fourth* station is a **bunting station**, where hitters can practice both sacrifice bunts and bunts for base hits. As we said before, bunting is too often neglected. Most of the hitters we see, as coaches, can't bunt. Bunting is a great weapon when used properly. It should be incorporated into your practice.

The *fifth* station is the **pepper station**. A pepper station is composed of a hitter and three or four fielders arranged in a semicircle of about 10 feet who throw soft pitches to the hitter. The hitter taps the pitches back to the fielders, alternating to whom he hits in some type of order or in random order.

Pepper is an excellent routine for hitters to practice the idea of the bat being an extension of the hand. Hitters should try to control the location of the pitches by moving their hands and body to simulate inside or outside pitches. They should also try to direct their hits to the right, middle, or left and hit both line drives and ground balls. In addition to enhancing hand/eye coordination, improving bat control, and revealing the dominant hand, pepper also develops defensive skills on the part of the fielders at the same time.

These are the five stations that are recommended for practicing with young hitters. You may decide to use only two of them on a daily basis, depending on how many players you have and how many are present at a particular practice. In one practice, you might use only live hitting and whiffle balls. The next time you might want to use live hitting, whiffle balls, and bunt stations. Again, vary the activity to avoid "practice boredom." The general rule of thumb in practice sessions is that players hit after they do their defensive work. Periodically, however, it is important to hit first in practice when players are fresh and ready to go.

Figure 2 shows how a practice might be organized using some of the stations.

There are a few key points to keep in mind regarding hitting practice. It is critical that the hitter be loose and in a proper frame of mind before he ever takes his first swing. What can help is to cover in the first five minutes all the

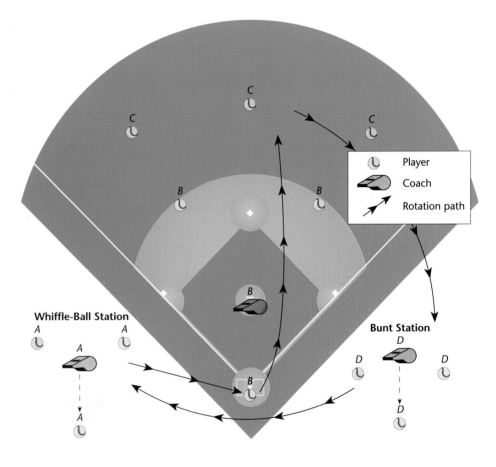

**FIGURE 2**
*An example of station-work organization.*
*Players rotate from one station to the next, preferably from whiffle ball to live hitting, since that allows the players to loosen up first. The pepper station can be added or replaced for variety.*

*This setup is based on a 12-player team with 3 coaches. A sample rotation is:*

  *Group A: (Whiffle ball) rotates to live hitting.*
  *Group B: (Live hitting) rotates to fielding.*
  *Group C: (Fielding) rotates to bunt station (or pepper station).*
  *Group D: (Bunt) rotates to whiffle ball (or tee station).*

## For The Advanced Hitter.............................................

*For most hitters, one hand is generally stronger than the other. While at the pepper station, have the player work choking up or using either a shortened or a lighter bat. He can then play one-handed pepper, first with one hand and then with the other. The goal is to see which hand, if any, is stronger or more dominant. Hand injuries are the most dreaded enemy of a hitter at higher levels of play. Knowing which hand is dominant can be invaluable if the hitter ever has an injury to one hand and must compensate by greater use of the other hand.*

*For major leaguers who throw right and bat left, or throw left and bat right, the throwing hand is the bottom hand on the bat. Thus it tends to be dominant, creating a slight advantage.*

fundamentals as well as pitch counts before they even begin taking a cut at a baseball.

To cover depth and distance, get an old piece of indoor/outdoor carpeting. Cut each player a section in the same dimensions as the plate. Have the players use these carpet plates to check their depth and distance. Then take five minutes to go back through all the hitting fundamentals, including depth and distance, setting the stance, forming a box, and using the 45-degree angle. Cover the systematic approach to hitting *every* single day before the hitters swing the bat. The goal is to ingrain these habits into the players' muscle memory so that they

will be used almost instinctively in a live game.

Once you have them thinking about the fundamentals of hitting, take hitters 13 and older into pitch counts. Start with an 0–0 count. What is the hitter looking for? Is he looking for a fastball in his favorite hitting zone? What about a 1–0 count? Now he is definitely looking for a fastball in his favorite zone! Cover the 2–0, 3–0, and 3–1 counts with the emphasis on hitting high percentage pitches: fastballs or the pitch that the hitter prefers and the pitcher tends to throw for strikes. Work on the 0–2 count as well, asking the player to hit anything close to the strike zone.

Next, stress being aggressive at the plate. The hitter should plan on swinging at a pitch right up to the point at which he can tell whether it is a ball, rather than waiting to identify the pitch before deciding whether or not to swing. For most hitters, there is simply not time to do the latter. It is better to start a swing and stop it than to stop a swing and then start it! Emphasize that while you want the hitter to swing at strikes, it is better that he take an aggressive swing at a bad pitch than no swing at all.

It is such a temptation, especially at levels where pitchers have trouble throwing strikes, to press a weak hitter to take pitches. Very often, unaggressive hitters decide on their own or are told by the coach to take the first pitch. Suppose, though, that that particular pitch is the best one during that time at bat. The hitter is then immediately in a hole on the count and is drawn into the act of swinging at bad pitches. If a pitch is good, swing at it! Not swinging takes the fun of a base hit away from weak hitters and deprives them as well of the opportunity to develop their hitting confidence and skills. Such tactics can eventually drive the player out of the game. Hitters need to swing at the ball in order to develop!

In working with pitch count situations with older hitters, you might choose to be the pitcher and start, for example, on an 0–0 count and go into the windup. Ordinarily, once the pitcher shows his hip pocket to the hitter, the hitter shows his hip pocket and the pitcher calls the pitch. The call might be a fastball away or a fastball down the middle, a curveball away or a curveball down the middle, or a hanging curveball. In this case,

"Be aggressive at the plate. The hitter should plan on swinging at a pitch right up to the point at which he can tell whether it is a ball, rather than waiting to identify the pitch before deciding whether or not to swing. For most hitters, there is simply not time to do the latter. It is better to start a swing and stop it than to stop a swing and then start it! While coaches want their hitters to swing at strikes, it is better that hitters take an aggressive swing at a bad pitch than no swing at all. If a pitch is good, swing at it!"

however, you call the pitch, put the hitter in a count, tell him what the pitch is, and force him to think through it. You will be helping the hitter begin to develop the *mental* fundamentals of hitting. It takes only five minutes and will do the hitter a world of good.

In summary, each day during the few minutes of loosening up re-emphasize all the fundamentals of hitting, both physical and mental. Make sure to cover the pitch counts. You and your players will reap high dividends as the season moves on.

## Situational Hitting

The best way to teach situational hitting is to run actual situations, both defensively and offensively at the same time. Having one player at bat and all others merely standing around is not an effective use of anyone's time. In practicing situational hitting, change players from offense to defense. In a short period of time, each hitter then gets a lot of swings while at the same time practicing his defensive skills.

You can do situational hitting in a pre-planned manner or you might vary the practice by trying a hit and run for hitters aged 13 to 15. You might also ask your players to try to drive in a run from third base with less than two outs or just try to move a runner over. Another possibility is a sacrifice bunt to advance a base runner. Any number of situations can be drilled.

Situational hitting for hitters 13 and older also can be practiced by incorporating it into live hitting, that is, the hitting that is done in normal practice on a field or in a batting cage. When the hitter comes to the plate, use the following routine:

- On the first pitch, try a sacrifice bunt to first base. Put a runner on first, but do not have him advance yet.
- On the second pitch, ask for a sacrifice bunt to third.
- On the third pitch, try a hit and run. The base runner takes off and the hitter's job is to hit the ball to the opposite side on the ground and execute the hit and run.
- On the next pitch, assume less than two outs and move the runner from second to third. You may, if you wish, take a practice pitch in between so the base runner can catch his breath. Remember that the object is to move the runner from second to third. If a right-handed hitter is up, he will try to hit the ball the other way. If a left-handed hitter is up, he will try to pull the ball to right field to get the runner from second to third.
- Then try a squeeze bunt.
- Then let the hitter swing away.
- Ask for a base hit to left center and then one to right center.
- Some options for scoring a runner from third base are as follows. Consider a situation with less than two outs. The goal of the hitter is a flyball deep enough to score the runner, a sacrifice fly, or a base hit. If the middle infield is back, the hitter can hit a hard ground ball to second or the shortstop that will score the runner from third as well.

Some of the possibilities will depend, of course, on the situation. If the hitter wants to add some variety to the situation, pull the infield in. That is the easiest time to hit. If the hitter gets a pitch he can drive, he should hit it hard because, when the infielders are in, their reaction time is diminished. Some say that this can add .100 points to the hitter's batting average.

In the last six or seven swings, have the hitter practice swinging away and hitting the ball hard. But be careful! What the hitter should *not* do, especially with a slow batting-practice pitcher, is try to hit the last six or seven balls out of the ballpark. Inevitably, when that hitter gets into an actual game, the pitcher will be faster and he will either pop up the first couple of times at bat or strike out. A way to prevent such overswinging is to give the batter only two or three additional pitches. Then for each line drive, allow him another swing.

Allow each hitter to run out the last hit ball. Get him to first base and leave him there so that he can see the results of what he has done. This gives the players the opportunity to work on base-running skills as well as hitting skills.

The value of situational hitting is that on almost every given pitch, the hitter has an opportunity to work on a different situation. He can think about the pitch and learn to change gears from one situation to another very rapidly. This drill gives the hitter no chance to let down or become mentally lazy.

## Enhancing Competition

Another way you can spice up the situational hitting is to divide the team into groups of four. If there are twelve players, have eight players in the field and four hitting. Whenever someone executes something properly, give the team a point. Add up the points at the end of practice and give the winning group some type of award—maybe soft drinks after practice or a few extra swings. Whatever the reward, it makes the practice fun and provides some competition at the same time.

Competing for rewards can motivate interest in a practice session that the players might otherwise consider boring. For example, compete with the players for a soft drink—you against the entire team. Or keep a pocketful of sugarless bubble gum for the younger players. When a player executes a skill, flip him a piece of gum.

In situational hitting with runners on base, let the players compete, either with four-man teams or as individuals. Switch the routine periodically. Every now and again, get the whiffle balls out and have a competition. For example, give each player on the team five swings. Whoever hits the ball the hardest the greatest number of times wins. Buy the winner(s) a soft drink or milkshake after practice.

Older players at the varsity level in either high school or college do not need as much motivation. These players are generally well focused—most high school players want to play in college and most college players want to play professionally. Although their goal may be clear, however, it is important to motivate them from time to time by giving them something to shoot for. Any time that you provide additional competition, you place hitters in a situation in which they are forced to concentrate. Such enhanced concentration is important. Lack of concentration will get a hitter in trouble more quickly than just about anything.

Another way to compete is with bunting—a neglected area of practice.

"Any time that you provide additional competition, you place hitters in a situation in which they are forced to concentrate. Such enhanced concentration is important. Lack of concentration will get a hitter in trouble more quickly than just about anything."

Put a couple of helmets about two or three feet from the foul lines. Then give each hitter an opportunity to bunt four or five times to see if he can get the bunt down and into a helmet rather than right back at the pitcher. Reward the winner by letting him lead the running.

As you watch hitters, particularly those in college, play pepper, you will notice that they are always in competition, and always have something at stake. For example, if the defensive player misses the ball, he has to move to the end of the line. If the hitter hits a ball that is caught in the air, his hitting time is over.

Another way to introduce competition with pepper is to give points. For example, a defensive player gets two points if he catches a pop-up and one point if he catches a line drive; an offensive player gets one point for hitting a line drive. The first player to get 11 points is the winner. A swing and miss is an out and the defense gets 11 points. Errors by fielders send a game back to 0. If the defense gets 11 points before the hitter, he goes to defense and a new hitter starts out. If the hitter gets 11 points before the defense, he gets to hit again. This is constant competition.

Players like constant competition; in fact, they thrive on it. This competitive nature is often what attracts them to the game. It stands to reason, then, that competition can enhance a practice. In the game of baseball, a player must deal with failure on a second-by-second basis. If he cannot do so effectively, then he will not succeed. The successful baseball player has learned through competition to be mentally tough.

# Practice Organization for Teams

## Station Work

1. Live hitting: field or cage
2. Tee work: backstop or porta-sock
3. Whiffle ball: two or three players
4. Bunting station: sacrifices and hits
5. Pepper station: three or four players

## Situational Hitting

1. Offense and defense together
2. Run hitters in and out
3. Work situations
   a) Sacrifice bunt to first
   b) Sacrifice bunt to third
   c) Hit and run
   d) Move runner from second to third with less than two outs.
   e) Squeeze bunt
   f) Score runner from third with less than two outs.
   g) Swing away
   h) Extra base hits to left center and right center
   i) Hitter becomes base runner
   k) Score runner
4. Divide team into groups of four.

## Enhance Competition

- By rewards
- By situational hitting with four-man teams
- By competing with bunting situations
- By using pepper

# CHAPTER SEVEN

# Approaches to Hitter Development

1. Ages 4–7
2. Ages 8–10
3. Ages 11–12
4. Ages 13–15
5. Ages 16–18
6. Ages 18 and Older

**Jeff.** The story involves a player I coached at Southport High School. When he was a sophomore, he batted .168. When he was a junior, he batted .189. After the season ended in the spring, I had to be honest with him regarding his status for the upcoming senior year, that his chances of playing much the following season were very small. That conversation lit a fire under him. During the following summer, fall, and winter, he dedicated himself to baseball improvement.

He set up a batting tee and rug in his garage and took 150 swings a day, increased his bench press from 125 pounds to 225 pounds, and arrived at spring practice in mid-season condition. Not only did his batting average increase to .375, but he went from not playing at all, to ninth in the batting order, to leadoff by the end of the season. He had never hit a home run in his high school career, but hit three during his senior year.

The team won the county championship and went on to win the sectional and regional championships and then made it to the final sixteen teams in the state championships.

I will always be proud of the accomplishments of this player. It taught me to never underestimate what a person can achieve when he dedicates himself to improvement.

A pproaches to hitter development vary according to the age and the maturity of the individual player. In this chapter we discuss an appropriate approach for each of six age levels: (1) 4–7; (2) 8–10; (3) 11–12; (4) 13–15; (5) 16–18; and (6) over 18. The factors that vary among these approaches are coaching intensity, level and difficulty of exercises and weight training, types of drills used, aspects of the game to be emphasized, and dedication and commitment to the game.

## (1) Ages 4–7

When working with young hitters, it is easy to want to "overcoach," pushing them to accomplish a little more than their abilities or motivation allow. This is, of course, not a malicious attempt by any parent or coach. It is only natural to want our children to be as excited about baseball as we are. This enthusiasm, however, makes it difficult to curb our desire to immediately transfer our knowledge and love of the game to the players.

With children aged 4–7, the game will be, for the most part, merely a recreational activity. For this reason, it is important to approach baseball, and hitting in particular, in a very non-threatening way. The players must have fun at what they are doing. There is no need for any pressure at this age level. Every ounce of feedback that you provide the children must be positive. Though attempts should be made to correct mistakes, at this age, all criticism should be constructive, and not negative. If playing baseball ceases to be fun, you will run the risk of driving the children from the game—a sad result. Children at this age easily become disinterested in anything that is not associated with having fun. Be sure to temper your approach to coaching and teaching hitting with this in mind.

Practice should be encouraged but not forced. Adults have a tendency to want to head for the backyard after work to play catch or hit. In many cases, that is not what children want to do. They might prefer to watch cartoons, play video games, ride a bike, or finish a game with a friend. It is important not to push children into practice and then show your frustration when they express disinterest. Is it the child who wants to play or the parent? Let your children adopt their own schedules, if any. When they are ready to practice, they will let you

know. You can encourage them by asking, "Do you want to go out and play catch or hit?" If they open the door to you, be prepared to give them your best, even if it may not be at a time most convenient for you, but *don't push them*!

If approached correctly, working with hitters aged 4–7 can give youngsters a great head start. Please understand that the routine we suggest will not necessarily apply to all players. Some children will be much more in tune with baseball than others. While some will spend 3 hours a day at baseball at age 5, others may be willing to spend only 3 minutes. So, be careful to adjust and adapt our suggested routine to the individual player.

Two points need to be emphasized when working with this age level. First, this is the appropriate time to begin teaching the fundamentals. Thus it is important that you understand the fundamentals as well, so that you can begin teaching using a very slow, but methodical process. Cover one or two points a day and continue to review and emphasize the fundamentals as you go along. No matter how bright the child, he will still have a tendency to forget what he has been learning

San Francisco Giants/Martha Jane Stanton

without constant reinforcement. He will then begin to both remember and understand each of the fundamentals and how important they are to building his skills.

Second, players aged 4–7 should take 25–50 swings per day 2–4 days per week. Once again, the actual number depends on the interest level of the hitter. This can be accomplished in many ways other than spending time and money on a batting machine. For example, the use of golf whiffle balls, as we explained in Chapter 6, makes possible a simple practice drill that is inexpensive and does not require a great deal of time. At most, the investment is around $2.50 for 12 whiffle balls, and without much effort, you can get 50 cuts in only 5 minutes a day. This is also a nonthreatening activity, unlike the batting cage or live hitting. Whiffle balls also give the hitter the opportunity to hit indoors during the winter, say, in a garage or basement.

Because they are easy to throw accurately, whiffle balls also allow you to give the hitter quality pitches. This in turn means that the hitter gets more quality swings than if you were pitching live balls from a greater distance.

"Parents should remember that hitting a baseball may be one of the hardest things to do in any sport. Because of this, the parents and the child must work together to keep from getting frustrated right at the beginning if things do not work out. It is going to take practice and patience. Try to get the child in a comfortable stance and spend a lot of time on fundamentals."

Robby Thompson, San Francisco Giants

If you are pitching to a hitter aged 4–7, you should consider pitching underhand. Be aware, however, that some of these players will become ready for overhand pitching by the age of 6 or 7. To be sure that the hitter is ready before doing so, you might try pitching whiffle balls overhand but from a kneeling position.

Many parents ask, "What can we do for our children to help them improve their strength or get them ready to play, whether it be baseball or any other sport?" We list some exercises that we have found successful with young hitters. We suggest 10–15 situps and 10–15 pushups 2 or 3 times per week. Be sure to encourage the hitters when they are able to accomplish the goal. We also suggest using some isometric exercises, many of which you can learn from a qualified weight instructor. Another recommended exercise is the simulated bench press. The player, without weights, acts as though he is doing a bench press. The exertion is created when you resist his hands as he lifts. We also encourage the following triceps exercise: Hold the child's elbow and bend his arm. As he straightens out his arm, work the triceps. Do this with both arms. Since you are providing the resistance, you can control it as well, being careful not to apply so much pressure that an injury might occur.

It is important that all parents and coaches understand that during this age period, you are beginning to lay the foundation not only for hitting fundamentals but also for a basic work ethic. Remember: It can be fun when a player works hard and sees improvement. As we mentioned earlier, you should ask only two things of your players: Listen to your coach or instructor and give your best effort. If the player cannot do both of these, he is better off not even attempting the task.

## (2) Ages 8–10

By the time a child is 8–10 years old, an evolutionary process has taken place. His attention span has greatly increased, allowing him to absorb a lot more information. Nevertheless, it remains important that you make almost everything fun. Moreover, you want to ensure that all feedback is of a positive nature. Whenever a player makes a mistake, it should be pointed out, but in an encouraging manner rather than one that is harsh or critical.

Working hard and seeing improvement can be fun. The game of baseball must not be drudgery, but rather something the child can look forward to—a game he plays rather than something he must work at. This does not mean that you should not get after players occasionally for loafing. What it *does* mean is that you must strike a delicate balance between fun and work.

**"We caution parents and coaches against the temptation of expecting perfection. Children 8–10 years old are not going to give you perfection."**

Once again be sure to let your players know that you expect them to listen and give their best effort when they are practicing. If they can do that for only 5 minutes, then use that 5 minutes each day. If they can do so for 20 or 30 minutes, then all the better. It is important, however, that they realize that this is critical to ensure their progress.

We caution parents and coaches against the temptation of expecting perfection. None of us is perfect and certainly children will make mistakes. Children at this age level often cannot concentrate and will drift off mentally. This behavior is not unusual and is certainly no reflection on your coaching ability. If you keep your expectations realistic, your time with them will be spent more profitably.

As with any age group, it is important that you constantly reinforce the fundamentals. At this stage, they will begin to develop many lifelong habits: both good *and* bad. Thus, in order to emphasize the good habits, challenge them to memorize the fundamentals—to know them and perform them. Playing baseball has its own intrinsic satisfaction, but an occasional tangible reward for doing things well at this stage in their development can be effective. You might try something as simple as a piece of gum or maybe a soft drink or a milkshake. If you cannot impress the importance of learning the fundamentals by talking, then try the reward system. It will pay off in the long run.

Fear of the ball is an issue that must be seriously addressed at this age level.

Generally, hitters begin seeing live pitching from fellow players at about the age of 8. Such pitching can be a very traumatic experience. Hitters must adjust from a coach, whose pitching they trust, to a pitcher their own age, who in many cases does not have any idea where the ball is going. Often players are hit by a pitch, and such an experience is not easily forgotten. It takes some time and effort to help a hitter at this age overcome his fear of the ball. If you remember all those times that you went to the plate afraid, you can perhaps appreciate how some of your players feel.

First, it is important to be honest and let them know that they *will* be hit by a pitch *at some point* in their baseball career. Explain that although you have been hit by a pitch, you continue to play. Statistics show that a hitter has about a 1 out of 50 (or 2 percent) chance of being hit by a pitch. But point out that this also means that the chance of *not* being hit is 49 out of 50 (or 98 percent)! Keep stressing that players go through entire seasons and are never hit by a pitch.

To deal with the fear of being hit, we suggest that you work with your players in two ways. The biggest fear the hitter has is being hit in the face, so first, use the following technique to reinforce his ability to move out of the way. Take 4 or 5 tennis balls and position the hitter at the plate. Tell him that you will occasionally try to hit him and that you want him to try to get out of the way. Locate the first pitch right down the middle. Then throw the second or third pitch at him. Do not throw hard but do throw it *at* him, keeping in mind that it is difficult to be hurt by a tennis ball. Then locate a pitch down the middle again. Then throw another one at him. After 5 or 6 pitches have been thrown at him, he will discover that nearly every time he is able to get out of the way.

Second, teach them the best position to be in if they are unfortunate enough to be hit. We covered this earlier in Chapter 3 (see Figure 15). Most important, they must turn their face away from the ball. The hitters most likely to actually be hurt are those who freeze when the ball comes toward their face. Have the hitter turn his face away from the pitcher, drop the bat head to the ground, and bend over so that when the ball comes at him, the only body parts that are exposed are the lower part of the back, the hips, and the back of the legs. His face is then out of the way and since the bat is down, he cannot be called on a cheap strike if the ball hits the bat. The force of gravity, when dropping the bat to the ground, also tends to speed up their getting out of the way. This drill can become a part of your daily practice routine.

The practice routine for children aged 8–10 is similar to the routine for those aged 4–7 except that the pace is increased. One very important drill from Chapter 4 should be added—Drill #6: Bat Behind the Back—which will help the player form the habit of using the back foot and the hips. We recommend 10 repetitions of this drill daily, for about 2 minutes 3 or 4 times per week.

We also suggest 50 swings 3 or 4 times per week. If the hitters are willing to do more, all the better, but remember not to push them too hard. During live batting practice, be sure to throw overhand pitches since the pitchers they will now face will throw in that manner. We suggest that if you are using a routine of 50 swings, at least a portion of the time should be spent with whiffle balls. Whiffle balls should be incorporated into every

baseball practice from the age of 4 on to the college level. They provide some unique benefits, not the least of which is that a great deal of hitting can be accomplished in a short period of time. Their use also allows 3 or 4 players to get additional cuts at good pitches and work on their fundamentals while the other players are hitting live.

Regarding live hitting using batting machines, one caution is in order. The pitching machine at a batting cage is fine so long as it throws pitches that are similar to what your hitters are seeing. It obviously does an 8- or 9-year-old hitter no good to experience 60-mph pitches. All this will accomplish is scaring the hitter. If he hits a pitch on the handle or off the end of the bat, stinging his hand, he may no longer want to swing at all, and the purpose of the practice is defeated. If you can find a batting cage at which the ball is thrown anywhere from 30 to 40 mph, and your players are not afraid to step in and hit, then let them do so. *Never* force a hitter into a cage if he fears the ball.

Be creative when using the batting cage. One of the first warnings a pitcher receives when learning to pitch is to keep from grooving the pitches to the same place over the plate. This gives us a clue for working with a batting machine. Move *forward* to work on fast pitches and bat quickness. Move *backward* to work on slower pitches and staying back on the swing. Move *away* from the plate to work on outside pitches. Move *close* to the plate to work on inside pitches.

For the 8–10-year-old, use the same exercise routine mentioned earlier for 4–7-year-olds, but increase the number of situps to 25–30 per day and pushups to 12–18 per day. Add Drill #18, Iso Bat, to the isometric exercises as well. This isometric drill is designed to improve and increase hitting skills through a regular swinging motion. The hitter positions the bat where he would be making contact with the pitch directly over the middle of the plate. Once the bat is there and the back foot is rolled up, provide resistance for the hitter by simply putting your hand on the bat and resisting him as he makes the swing. As he gets to the point of contact, he will continue his swing as you resist all the way to complete follow-through. Be careful not to resist him so much that he must change his normal swinging motion. In other words, you do not want him to have to bend his arms and force the bat through. A nice and easy swing is

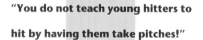

**"You do not teach young hitters to hit by having them take pitches!"**

the objective. You will be surprised at just how rapidly hitters improve their strength with this particular drill. It should be performed at least 5, but not more than 10 repetitions 2 to 3 times per week.

At this age level, it is also appropriate to begin stressing aggressiveness at the plate. This is a point we have made several times throughout the book. You do not teach young hitters to hit by having them take pitches!

## (3)  Ages 11–12

For this age group, we would rather have hitters become overly aggressive with the bat than become passive and take too many pitches. Again, hitters learn to swing by taking their cuts. The batter should go to the plate physically and mentally ready to swing at every pitch. Then he adjusts according to the pitch. Explain that it is better to start a swing and stop if the pitch is bad, rather than wait to see if the pitch is a ball or strike and then mentally and physically prepare to swing. The 0.4 second it takes for the pitch to get to the plate simply does not allow the luxury of such passiveness.

At this age level, you can begin to diagnose specific weaknesses and make suggestions and recommendations for drills that will help or correct those weaknesses. Up to age 10, we stressed the fundamentals. With ages 11–12, you should make sure the players are accomplished enough in their fundamentals that both you and the hitter together can begin to pick out specific strengths and weaknesses. You can then concentrate on troubleshooting and fine-tuning the swing, which will now become a constant battle, regardless of how far the hitters progress. Even those who make it all the way to the major leagues continue to troubleshoot and fine-tune their hitting skills with the aid of their coaches.

In certain sports, such as Olympic gymnastic competition, there are many athletes (girls, in particular) who excel at a very young age because they have been trained from the age of 4 or 5 to compete. By the age of 11–13, these athletes are able to compete on a national level. Although athletes do not mature in baseball at the age of 11 or 12, the need for early training and constant reinforcement of the fundamentals is the same.

For players in this age group, certain drills should be used routinely for nearly every player. Each of these has been covered in Chapter 4. The first is Drill #3: Right/Left/Middle, which works on inside and outside pitches and hitting the ball to right, left, and center fields. Although this skill is an important one, coaches often tend to overlook it, allowing players to hit the ball strictly to one part of the field while ignoring the other fields. Whatever type of hitter he happens to be, it is still important that the hitter know how to handle pitches over all parts of the plate.

In fact, as hitters get older, the better hitters get fewer and fewer good pitches to hit. Pitchers tend to work hitters much more toward the outside of the plate. In fact, 67 percent of all pitches for strikes are over the outside half of the plate and 33 percent are over the inside half of the plate. Most pitches over the middle of the plate are mistakes. A player who can hit an inside pitch only to the pull side of the field has decreased his effectiveness, perhaps by as much as 67 percent.

Keep in mind the following when using the Right/Left/Middle drill. On the inside pitch, try to emphasize quick hips. On the outside pitch, emphasize these four points. One, the hitter must have a good back foot, squishing the bug and rotating his hips. Two, the hitter must have a strong top hand. If his top hand is a bit lazy or slow, a poor bat angle is created and he will tend to pop the ball up or completely

miss it. Three, the hitter must keep his head down in order to make sure that he sees the ball on the outside part of the plate. If his head comes up, the front shoulder will almost certainly come up off the ball, which eliminates any chance of hitting it. Four, the hitter must keep his hands inside the ball, that is, driving the hands down and inside the ball to hit it to the opposite field.

It is beneficial to teach players at this age level how to differentiate between a high pitch and a low pitch. The hitter must learn to study the pitcher's release points, in the same way he watches a thrower's release points when playing catch, to see whether

### To hit an outside pitch to the opposite field, the hitter must:

1. have a good back foot, squishing the bug and rotating the hips,
2. have a strong top hand,
3. keep his head down,
4. drive the hands down and inside the ball.

the pitch is high or low. The body re-acts a little differently to each release point. Use Drills #10 and #11, Low Pitch and High Pitch, respectively from Chapter 4. Early on, start the drills with a tee, raising the tee to a point that would simulate a high pitch. If at all possible, use a two-part

"In fact, as hitters get older, the better hitters get fewer and fewer good pitches to hit. Pitchers tend to work hitters much more toward the outside of the plate."

tee, taking the top part off and leaving only the bottom part on to simulate a low pitch. Be concerned about having the player get a little bit of flex in the front knee to go down and get the low pitch. The player should concentrate on keeping his head down and drop-ping the bat to the ball. The force of gravity can help with a swing at a low pitch because it allows the hitter to in-crease bat speed. Since the head of the bat is where most of its weight lies, let the bat head take advantage of the force of gravity. As discussed in the high-pitch drill, the hitter does not

flex the front knee. He just takes his normal stride and swings. Give the hitters the opportunity to work on both types of pitches.

Drill #9, Game Time, is another drill that works very well with this age group. It involves placing hitters in game situations and giving them the opportunity to compete against the coach, who is *both* the judge and the umpire. For example, begin the first inning with nobody on and nobody out and pitch with a regular count. If the hitter hits the ball hard and you think it would be a base hit, call a man on first and no outs. If the hitter pops up, determine whether it would be to the shortstop or second base and whether it would be caught. Chal-lenge the hitters. Give them some-thing to work for. Tell the team that if they can score 4 runs off you in 6 in-nings, you will buy them each a soft drink.

Other drills recommended for this age group are Drill #4: 1-2-3-4, Drill #15: 1-2-3, and Drill #17: Hip Thrust. Their use should be based, however, primar-ily on the individual needs of your hit-ters. A hitter may be weak in some areas and very strong in others, and the choice of drills must reflect this.

Once again be sure to use the batting cage appropriately, not only for pitch speed but also for varying positions. Be sure that you are aware of the speed of the pitches in the cage and that the hitters are making good, consistent contact while changing position in order to improve their work on fast, slow, inside, and outside pitches.

In a practice routine for 11–12-year-olds, increase the number of repetitions and the amount of time spent. Each hitter should do 15 repetitions of the Bat-Behind-the-Back drill, which will take only 2 or 3 minutes, 3 or 4 times per week. He should also take 50 swings, 4 or 5 times per week. This can be done with live pitching or whiffle balls, whichever you feel is most needed. In order to enhance understanding, this drill can also be done in front of a mirror with only the bat.

The exercise routine should now be expanded to 30–40 situps, 20–25 pushups, and 15–20 repetitions of the isometric exercises (especially the iso-bat drill) 2 or 3 days per week. A new routine to incorporate is having players squeeze a half rubber ball when they watch television or ride in a car. The ball should be small enough to fit into their hand and take some effort

**FIGURE 1**
*The wrist-roller device.*

to squeeze. The rubber ball is cut in half to help line up the fingers and see when the fingers and thumb come together. An alternative is to use either Silly Putty or hand grips.

For the youngster a little more dedicated to improving, you might set up a wrist roller. Take an old broom handle or piece of dowel 1 inch in diameter and cut a section about 1 to 2 feet long. Drill a hole at a perpendicular angle through the middle of the dowel. Then take a piece of rope, probably 3 to 4 feet long, and tie one end through a 3- to 5-pound weight or a brick. (An older player might use more

weight.) Then thread the other end through the hole in the dowel and tie securely. Place the weight on the ground and put the cord through a hook on a shelf above the weight and tie it through the dowel. See Figure 1.

Keeping the arms straight out in front, the player then rolls the dowel in his hands until the weight has rolled all the way up to the handle and then rolls it all the way down. It is important that the hitter not bend his arms at all, forcing his forearms to do the work. At one point in his career, Dan Driessen of the Cincinnati Reds used this exercise to come back from a wrist–forearm injury.

## (4) Ages 13–15

This age group may very well be the most difficult to play in and be successful. For that reason, we tend to lose as many or more players in this age group as we do in any of the others. The demands of baseball tend to conflict with the maturing processes of puberty and society. Up through age 12, Mom or Dad might have pushed a child to play. By this time as well, most young women have gravitated from baseball to softball.

By age 13, children either like baseball or do not. Often they do not because they have not had much success, may not have been coached properly, do not want to work hard to improve, or simply do not like the game. It's no fun to never get a hit or lose every game. During this period, a player normally makes a decision as to whether he wants to play baseball on a serious level or just likes it as a recreational activity. Thus this is often the most critical time for a hitter in terms of his eventual success.

**"The 13–15 age group may very well be the most difficult to play in and be successful. For that reason, we tend to lose as many or more players in this age group as we do in any of the others."**

If the player truly wants to improve and enjoy success, it is time to establish a stronger work ethic toward the game. There must be a dedicated effort toward *perfecting* all the fundamentals taught up to this point. Such an effort in baseball is no different than in school subjects or any other aspect of life. Probably the most critical aspect of perfecting the fundamentals is being able to recognize mistakes and knowing how to correct them. What a coach strives for with hitters in this age group is to keep from making the same mistake twice in a row.

When a hitter makes a mistake, try to help him recognize the mistake and get it corrected immediately. This should be done in practice, *not* in games, where there is already enough pressure on players. In a game, the hitter has the opportunity to do two things: (1) get a good pitch and (2) take a good cut. He is there to hit. It is usually wiser to diagnose problems and correct them *after* the game. In practice routines, however, strive to keep the hitter from making the same mistake twice.

Hitters aged 13–15 tend to let their minds wander and swing merely to swing. They are not concentrating on what they are doing or on what they need to do in order to improve. They just swing. It's important that you work with them to increase their level of concentration and decrease the amount of daydreaming.

You still want to be as positive as possible with the players. At this stage, however, you can begin to get on the players to be sure that you are getting their maximum effort. Although at younger ages this might drive a player away from the game, at this age, players are generally more committed to the game. Thus it is more reasonable that if you're not getting the expected effort, you can feel comfortable taking corrective action. This may take the form of extra work or just getting after a player to work harder to improve.

It is important to stress improving the ability of hitters to handle all kinds of pitches. At this age the pitchers start working the hitters, that is, they try different pitches, change speeds, move pitches to different parts of the strike zone, and try to get them to swing at bad pitches. Up to this point, pitchers had not really been in complete command of their pitches. Now they are improving somewhat. Not only will a pitcher locate pitches on different parts of the plate, but he may also throw an occasional curve ball or changeup. When facing a strong hitter, he may be asked by his coach to work the hitter on the outside of the plate. This will probably be a new experience for your hitters. Thus you

"Two coaches have been very inspirational to my career, and ironically they are both called Dusty. One is Dusty Rhodes, not the ex-Giant, but my junior college coach. He is now at the University of North Florida in Jacksonville. He was just tremendous. I can't say enough about him. He taught me to win and how to play hurt and provided a great base of fundamentals.

"The other is Dusty Baker. I'll remember these years with Dusty and what he has done for me the rest of my life. Now the things he has been teaching me are starting to click, even the mental part of hitting. Dusty has improved my mental outlook—thinking along with the game and getting an idea of the situation before you get up to the plate. He has had a tremendous impact, not just on hitting but on the total game. He is still trying to learn the game—in baseball you never know it all.

"I have been fortunate to have had good coaching from the time I was 11 years old right on up through high school, junior high, college, the minor leagues, and now in the majors."

Robby Thompson, San Francisco Giants

need to make them aware of where they might be pitched to, and then work with them on handling such pitches. This is a critical point for you as a coach. If you want hitters to learn to hit an outside pitch, for example, you must allocate practice time to deal with the task.

It is also important to begin introducing the philosophy of hitting the breaking pitch. The term "breaking pitch" is usually meant to imply a curveball, but in some baseball jargon it also includes sliders, sinkers, screwballs, forkballs, split-finger fastballs, and so on. If you want your hitters to hit a breaking pitch, you must spend time in practice working on it so that they know what to do. Often hitters will swing at a breaking pitch even though it may not even be close to the plate. The hitter must learn that there is another level of hitting beyond just swinging the bat—it involves using his mind. He makes a decision about what is pitched, where it is pitched, and how to react. He also needs to know how to make a correction when he reacts incorrectly. For more on hitting the breaking pitch, see Chapter 9.

At this level, the amount of time spent hitting during the practice routine should be increased. First of all, the hitter should do 20 repetitions of Drill #6: Bat Behind the Back, 3 or 4 times per week. Each set of 20 repetitions will take at most 2 or 3 minutes. During the season, he should also take 50–75 swings 4 or 5 times per week, which is 200–375 cuts per week at a minimum. Out of season, the best you can hope for is 50 swings 2 or 3 times per week. Once or twice a week during the season, include as well 5–10 minutes of specific drill time based on each hitter's individual needs. Any more than that is a bonus.

Other drills to maintain or add involve continuing work on the inside/outside pitches (Drill #3: Right/Left/Middle) and high/low pitches (Drills #10 and #11). Another effective drill that hitters always enjoy is Drill #9: Game Time.

At this level, players need to work on Drill #19: Counts and Situations. Spend some time training your hitters to deal with different counts, one right after another. For example, you might start with an 0–0 count. You throw the pitch and the batter takes it for a ball. Now the count is 1–0. How does altering the situation from 0–0 to 1–0 change the expectation of the hitter? You throw another pitch and the hitter takes it for ball 2. So now the count is 2–0. How does the hitter's expectation change from 1–0 to 2–0? It is very important that hitters begin to deal mentally with these kinds of changing counts. What is the hitter's expectation with a different starting count? With an 0–0 count, he is looking primarily for a fastball, a pitch that he can hit and hit hard. With a 1–0 count, his chances of seeing a fastball have increased, and his strike zone is tightened down a little bit. In other words, he does not have to swing at a pitch even though it may be a strike, because he is looking for a good pitch to hit. With a 2–0 count, he is looking not only for a certain fastball but also in a specific location. Insist that the hitter wait for a pitch in what is called the "box," probably a 12-inch–by–12-inch square. This box should be in a favorite area of the strike zone. Whether it be up, down, in, or out, the pitch should be one that can be hit hard and driven long. Tell him that if he does not get that pitch, he should let it go by. The worst he can do is end up with a 2–1 count.

Putting hitters into all types of count situations during practice eases the mental pressure when they are facing

**TABLE 1**

| Count Situation | Hitter's Pitch Expectation | Expected Batting Average |
|---|---|---|
| 0–1 | Fastball (good pitch to hit) | .318 |
| 0–1 | Pitcher's choice (stay away from 0–2) | .238 |
| 0–2 | Protect the plate (often a waste pitch) | .094 |
| 1–0 | Fastball (tighten strike zone) | .359 |
| 1–1 | Pitcher's choice (do not panic—get a good pitch to hit) | .282 |
| 1–2 | Protect the plate (put ball in play) | .166 |
| 2–0 | Fastball (great hitter's count) | .373 |
| 2–1 | Fastball (pitcher does not want to go to 3–1) | .366 |
| 2–2 | Pitcher's best pitch (protect the plate) | .316 |
| 3–0 | Fastball (pitch in hitter's best zone only) | .250 |
| 3–1 | Fastball (great hitter's count) | .365 |
| 3–2 | Typically fastball (be ready to hit—pitcher does not want a walk) | .263 |

the pitcher in a live game. Table 1 summarizes the hitter's expectations of the pitches on all possible count situations. The batting averages refer to what the hitter might expect to achieve—that is, the probability of success—in each situation. These data were compiled recently by the Arizona State University baseball team.

You should also practice hitting with base runners on certain bases. For example, put a runner on first base with no outs, and tell the hitter that his job is to move the runner to second base.

The hitter must get a pitch that he can drive and preferably keep off the ground, avoiding a double play. You can also put him in a hit-and-run situation where he is forced to swing or in a situation where there is a runner on third base with no outs. His job would then be to score the runner. Think up other kinds of situations that your players will benefit from and enjoy as well. More were explained in Drill #19, Counts and Situations, in Chapter 4.

Regarding the exercise routine for players aged 13–15, we want to caution you against involving a player in weight training too early, thus risking injury. The natural tendency is to rush work with free weights or weight machines. For the typical player, we think that the age of 14 is about the earliest advisable for beginning weight training, depending on his build and maturity. Make sure that a qualified weight instructor assists the player not only in lifting the weights but also in lifting them properly. Stress repetition rather than the amount of weight lifted. Every young person who goes into a weight room wants to lift as much as possible. Such activity, however, runs the risk of unnecessary injury and will not make the player a better hitter.

Thus it is important to make certain that players are always supervised either by you, if you are qualified, or by a weight instructor.

**"At the advanced level, good hitters generally have tight stomachs, strong legs, and especially strong thighs and hips."**

Those who are not mature enough to do the lifting should include in their exercise routine 50–75 situps and 25–30 pushups. Because the entire act of hitting is dependent on the stomach muscles, it is important to work on strengthening them. The stomach muscles aid in hip rotation. The center of strength and balance is up under and through the buttocks and into the stomach. At the advanced level, good hitters generally have tight stomachs, strong legs, and especially strong thighs and hips. We also recommend using isometric exercises such as the iso-bat drill, doing 10–15 repetitions 2 or 3 times per week, and 15–20 repetitions each of using a wrist roller and squeezing a ball. All these exercises should be done 4 or 5 times per week. Once the player forms the habit of doing them, they will not take very much time. If your hitters become accustomed to using these exercises as an enjoyable part of their training program and see results, the transition to weight training will be very easy.

## (5) *Ages 16–18*

At this level, the hitter, in conjunction with his parents and coaches, needs to determine his level of aspiration. If he has continued to play through the age of 16, he is most likely involved in high school baseball and has aspirations of being either a good high school player or going on to play college or professional baseball. If his dream is to be a Division I college player or a professional baseball player, then he must set goals now that will allow him to achieve those higher levels. The player needs to prepare accordingly, realizing that whatever he invests in himself leads directly to reward. If the player invests nothing, then he cannot expect to be a Division I player. It is just not going to happen. There is simply too much competitive talent.

It is our hope that in the preceding 8–10 years the hitter has developed the strong base of fundamentals that is essential for the future. Now he will begin to fine-tune any weaknesses. Often a hitter will tend to emphasize things he already does very well and avoid those that he does not. In reality, it should be just the other way around. He should continually focus his attention on what he does *not* do well.

Depending on the physical development of the hitter, you and he might begin to determine what type of hitter he will be. If he has not yet fully developed physically, then a re-evaluation may be appropriate later. We can divide hitters into three categories. One is the hitter who runs exceptionally well and can help the offense with his speed. Another is the average runner but good hitter with not a great deal of power—a line-drive, single, and double hitter. This hitter may develop into a power hitter as he matures physically. Finally, there is the power hitter, although in our experience they are few and far between. (That is why they are in such great demand at the major league level.) With all hitters, however, there is a continual need to stress the mechanics of good fundamental hitting.

**TABLE 2**

| Position in Lineup | Characteristics of Position |
| --- | --- |
| #1 | The job of the leadoff hitter is to get on base. To accomplish this means taking some pitches, acquiring good discipline with respect to the strike zone, and finding ways of getting on base. If a player can hit .225 as a leadoff hitter, but get on base 60 percent of the time, then he is doing a good job in that position in the order. For personal satisfaction, however, the hitter should strive for a higher batting average—say, .400. |
| #2 | This position requires the batter to hit behind the runner, take pitches to give the leadoff hitter an opportunity to steal second or third base, drop down sacrifice bunts, execute the hit and run, and hit the ball to the right side. Because this hitter must be willing to take pitches, he must handle the bat well with few strikeouts. |
| #3 | This position goes to the hitter with the best batting average, since he will come to the plate with lots of runners in scoring position. He should also be second or third on the team in terms of runs batted in (RBI's). |
| #4 | This player must be a strong hitter with the ability to drive in runs and to get important hits when needed. Good speed is also an asset at this position. |
| #5 | This player is very similar to the #4 hitter but may not be as consistent at producing RBI's. He must also be able to come through in the clutch. |
| #6 | The second leadoff man, this hitter is not quite as consistent as the #1 hitter but possesses good speed. |
| #7 | This player is similar to the #2 hitter. He must handle the bat well and be able to move runners up. |
| #8 | This player is probably the second weakest hitter, and one from whom you cannot expect a great deal. He should be able to bunt or hit the ball a long way, depending on his size and strength. Do your best to find a role for this hitter to fill and contribute in some way. |
| #9 | This player is the weakest hitter in the lineup. It is best if he has speed so that his ability to get on base gives the team two leadoff hitters, but you may not have this luxury. It is essential, however, that this hitter know how to bunt. |

At this point, the hitter must also make a decision about his position in the batting order. Such a determination is done by considering the role of hitters in the various spots in the batting order, as we see in Table 2.

It is important that each hitter fine-tune his ability to execute all phases of hitting. He will be called upon from time to time to hit and run, sacrifice bunt, provide a sacrifice fly, or lead off an inning and get on base. He will not be able to perform these tasks if he has not worked on these skills. That is why it is so critical that the proper foundation has been built at a younger age. Each individual high school program will be different. Some coaches like to bunt. Others like the hit and run. Some are very aggressive, whereas others are very conservative. It is important that the hitter develop his skills to the point where he can execute anything that is asked of him.

The hitter must consider as well that in about two years, he will be leaving his high school program. In most cases, high school coaches are proud to follow the careers of their graduating players, but they are not going on to college with the player! We have seen situations in high school where a player may hit fourth in the lineup merely because he is the best replica of a power hitter that the team has. He might then end up hitting leadoff when he moves on to college. This is, of course, not a conscious attempt by the high school coach to confuse the hitter, but rather a desire to make the most of the hitters he had available on that team. In college that particular hitter's role may change, because the college coach has players not only of greater talent, but of a wider variety of abilities as well. We have seen a high school ninth-position hitter move on to college and bat second in one year. At the college level, the hitter will have to assume even more responsibility for evaluating his abilities and ensuring that he can adapt to the next level of play.

The practice routine for hitters aged 16–18 is fairly strenuous. Many high school hitters think that whatever their coach provides them is enough. In nearly all cases, it is not. The typical high school coach does not have an assistant coach and thus must handle anywhere from 14 to 18 players by himself. He cannot possibly give each hitter enough hitting cuts in any given practice. It is important that the player assume some of the responsibility of developing his own skills. This may require additional practice time on his own, with a parent, other players, or a qualified hitting instructor in the area.

Throughout the season, hitters at this age level need to take a minimum of 75–100 cuts per day 5–7 days per week. Unless he is playing another sport, the hitter should get at least 50 cuts a day during the off-season as well. This might include shadow swinging with a fungo bat (a bat with a small barrel, normally used to hit ground balls to infielders). If whiffle balls are used, 50 cuts a day should take only about 5 minutes. Drills at this level should also be adapted to individual needs. If the hitter is having trouble with his back foot, for example, he needs to continue Drill #6: Bat Behind the Back. He must become adept at self-diagnosis, choosing the drills that he needs or likes and continuing to work on them.

In addition to proper rest and diet, it is also important at this age level that the hitter carry out a well-rounded weight-training program under the supervision of a qualified individual. Most high schools can provide such an instructor. If they cannot, then help can be found in local YMCAs and health clubs. The hitter may have to read books or gather information from other players or coaches in order to become informed about proper weight training. Strength and physical attributes are becoming more and more important in baseball. The old school of thought said that players should stay away from weight lifting because big, tight muscles might lead to a lack of the flexibility and agility needed for baseball. In recent years, however, colleges have moved away from that theory. All Division I college programs are heavily into weight training in order to prepare players physically for the rigors of a full season.

> "One caution is necessary regarding weight training! Be sure the weight training program is designed *for baseball* and not primarily for body building or heavy weightlifting. The hitter should not impair his flexibility and the full range of motion needed for hitting, throwing, and running."

One caution is necessary regarding weight training! Be sure the program is designed *for baseball* and not primarily for body building or heavy weightlifting. The hitter should not impair his flexibility and the full range of motion needed for hitting, throwing, and running.

An established exercise routine should supplement the hitter's expanded weight training, and he should continue the use of a wrist roller. Additional running is also beneficial to ensure that his legs are in condition to carry him through an entire season.

At the college level, players from the cold-weather states will face great competition in those from the sun-belt areas—that is, any warm-weather state in which baseball can be played virtually year-round. A player from Arizona, California, or Florida may play 100–150 games during the course of a year, whereas one from the Midwest or the Northeast may get in only 35–40 games per year. Thus, regardless of what the player might do in practice, if he lives in a colder climate, he is 60–100 games behind per year just in terms of time spent on the field and participation at a competitive level. This, of course, puts that

> To be competitive, players in cold-weather climates must make a special effort to work on baseball during the off-season.

player at a competitive disadvantage that is difficult to overcome, unless he makes a special effort to prepare properly. This is one reason why the Midwest is not as heavily scouted or recruited as the Sunbelt areas are.

We would certainly suggest to hitters who live in colder areas that they spend extra time during the winter working on baseball. Most players cannot just put down their glove in August, pick it back up in February, and expect to have a tremendous level of success in the spring. If not given constant attention, a player's level of play will drop off tremendously. We recommend that the player set up a way to hit in the garage—say, hitting tennis or whiffle balls into a net or tarpaulin. The player can also seek out indoor practice and teaching facilities in larger cities, as well as make more creative use of the gym and weight room in his high school.

## (6) Ages 18 and Older

Hitters aged 18 and older may be preparing for college (a junior college or a four-year school, NAIA, NCAA Division III, II, or I) or may be moving on to the minor leagues of professional baseball. Most are headed on to college. These players have spent the time and effort to be prepared and recruited by some college program. Consequently, the work ethic with these hitters is usually well grounded. Many, however, still lack a sense of direction. For those, the following information is prerequisite to their further development. The advanced hitter who aspires to professional baseball should read Chapter 9 as well.

College baseball has become very competitive, even at the junior college level. Be careful not to assume that competition at the junior college level is not as stiff because players were not good enough to enter a four-year school. Some junior college players may have selected that particular school due to its reputation for sending hitters into professional baseball. Some players who are actually four-year-college players may indeed be forced to attend a junior college because of poor grades or financial conditions. Whatever college a player attends, he will see better and better pitching and encounter players and coaches who have a much greater understanding of the game than in most high school programs. Thus he must prepare that much harder to keep pace.

Two keys determine success or failure at the college level. The first involves freshmen who generally do not possess the physical strength of the upperclassmen. They have the physical skills and attributes, but they cannot keep up with the traveling and physical demands associated with a 60-game schedule in a college-level program. It may take a young freshman a couple of years to develop physically to the point where he can compete with his own upper-class teammates. Thus it is critical that freshmen players spend a great deal of time in the weight room preparing physically to compete not only with their opponents but with their teammates as well.

The second key to success is for the hitter to get a great number of cuts. At the Division I level, hitters are getting at least 100 cuts per day and, in some cases, 200–300 swings per day by using tees, whiffle balls, soft-toss drills, and pitching machines. When Jeff Mercer coached at Indiana University, he often arrived at practice an hour early simply to throw extra batting practice. In some exceptional instances, hitters would stay after practice to hit. Those hitters were getting somewhere between 250 and 350 swings per day, 7 days per week. When a hitter uses this routine for several months of the year, he is at a disadvantage if he gives it up during the off-season. Nothing can replace that number of swings. Some of the success experienced by the Indiana University program at that time was due to ensuring that hitters got a lot of swings and perfected each specific area of hitting needed in game situations.

Our recommendation is taking a lot of swings, say, 100–200 per day. These swings can be done in several forms— live cuts, swings off the tee, whiffle balls, soft-toss drills, and certainly a combination of all of them. Drill #13: Short Screen, is an excellent alternative for getting a lot of swings at certain types of pitches, and it can be part of the hitter's routine of 100–200 swings per day. It is *imperative* that the hitter spend a great deal of time swinging the bat in order to prepare for the type of pitching he will see in the upcoming season.

"Our recommendation is taking a lot of swings, say, 100–200 per day. These swings can be done in several forms— live cuts, swings off the tee, whiffle balls, soft-toss drills, and certainly a combination of all of them."

The hitter must also concentrate on four other phases of hitting at this level: (1) the bunt for the base hit, (2) the sacrifice bunt, (3) the slash bunt, and (4) the push bunt. The slash bunt is achieved by squaring to bunt early, pulling the bat back into a hitting position, and finally swinging away, hoping to slap the ball for a hit past either the first or third baseman as he charges hard. It is used effectively by many college teams but rarely in high school programs. Thus it is generally new to first-year college baseball players. The push bunt involves hitting the normal bunt a bit harder, past the pitcher toward the second baseman. It is used most effectively against a left-handed pitcher who tends to fall off the mound toward third base during his delivery.

Since the college game tends to be more aggressive than the high school game, the hit and run becomes a much more popular tactic for coaches at this level. It will be used with men on first and second and on different pitch counts. Also used are any number of aggressive tactics, such as the double steal, not typically seen in high school, where coaches tend to be a bit more conservative due to the physical limitations of their players.

Appropriate drills should be determined by the player and his coach, but certainly the 20 drills discussed in Chapter 4 will serve the hitter well at the college level. By this time, the hitter should be aware of his problem areas, how to correct them, and how to combat them. Three hitters from the same high school program might be on different drill systems by virtue of their specific problems. One may have a problem with the back foot or an inward turn. Another may be a dead stop hitter. Still another may have a problem with the front shoulder releasing early. Dealing with specific combinations of these kinds of problems leads to customized drill combinations. The hitter should use the drills that he needs and that work best for him.

One advantage of moving into the college ranks is that typically there is an assistant coach to work only with the hitters. Since the sport has become more specialized at this level, usually there is an assistant who works with the hitters, one who works with the pitchers, and maybe even, at the Division I level, a coach who works with the infielders, the catchers, and the outfielders.

Coaching and playing at the college level is made easier by the fact that players are willing to pay the price and put forth the effort to be successful. If they are not, they probably would not have made it this far. Still, there will always be a couple of players on any team who feel that they will be successful just by showing up. Such is not the case. The most important message we convey in this section is that a player at the college level must *continue* to work hard simply because the pitching is better than any he will have encountered to this point.

No longer will the hitter face only one good pitcher out of five games. He is more likely to see three or four, depending on the level. The hitter must be prepared for this progression in pitching ability. Pitchers will be throwing pitches on counts that he may never have seen before, such as 2–0 curveballs or 3–1 changeups. The pitchers are more adept at getting these pitches over the plate. They use their heads. They are not just throwing fastballs hoping to get them over the plate. To be prepared to compete, the hitter must be in good physical and mental shape. If he is not, he will not be very successful. This is a different level and it needs to be approached as such. College-level baseball is the closest thing to a job that a hitter has before entering the real world. Also, the combination of academic life and athletic life is a difficult one to balance. If the player is not disciplined, he will not be successful.

The college player also begins to face other adjustments. The more he progresses, the more his ego can get deflated. He may no longer be the team star. Other nonbaseball adjustments might simply involve not being at home, not having his girlfriend nearby, or not being able to handle the rigors of college academics.

# Approaches to Hitter Development

| Age Level | Fundamentals | Swings | Exercises | Drills (See Chapter 4) |
|---|---|---|---|---|
| 4–7 | • Begin fundamentals.<br>• Listen to coach.<br>• Give best effort. | 25–50 per day, 2–4 days per week | 10–15 situps;<br>10–15 pushups;<br>isometrics;<br>simulated benchpress;<br>triceps exercise | |
| 8–10 | • Hammer home fundamentals.<br>• Work on dismissing fear of ball.<br>• Start stressing being aggressive at the plate. | 50 per day, 3–4 days per week | 25–30 situps;<br>12–18 pushups;<br>isometric exercises | #6: 10 reps 3–4 times per week;<br>#18 |
| 11–12 | • Have hitters be overly aggressive rather than passive.<br>• Start stressing work ethic. | 50 per day, 4–5 times per week | 30–40 situps;<br>20–25 pushups;<br>15–20 reps of isometric exercises;<br>hand exercises;<br>wrist rollers | #6: 15 reps 3–4 times per week;<br>#3; #4; #5; #7; #8; #9; #10; #11; #17;<br>#18: 10–15 reps 2–3 times per week |
| 13–15 | • Establish stronger work ethic.<br>• Recognize mistakes quicker and correct.<br>• Stress ability to handle all kinds of pitch locations as well as breaking balls. | 50–75 per day, 4–5 times per week | 50–75 situps;<br>25–30 pushups;<br>isometric exercises;<br>15–20 wrist rollers;<br>hand exercises.<br>Begin weight training for some 15-year-olds. | #6: 20 reps 3–4 times per week;<br>#3; #4; #5; #7; #8; #9; #10; #11; #17;<br>#18: 10–15 reps 2–3 times per week;<br>#19 |
| 16–18 | • Stress strong base in fundamentals.<br>• Determine aspiration level.<br>• Work on weaknesses.<br>• Begin to determine type of hitter.<br>• Be able to execute all phases of hitting.<br>• Establish off-season practice program. | 75–100 per day in season,<br>5–7 days per week;<br>50 cuts per day in off-season | Carry out a well-rounded weight program, use wrist rollers, and get in additional running. Develop proper diet and rest patterns. | Adapt to individual need. |
| 18 and older | • Stress strong base in fundamentals and well-grounded work ethic.<br>• Work on bunting and hit and run. | 100–200 per day | Emphasize weight training. Develop proper diet and rest patterns. | #13 helps in getting extra swings.<br>Work on drills #1–#20 as needed. |

# CHAPTER EIGHT

# The Hitter's Mind

1.  Physical–Mental Preparation Before Game Day

2.  Putting on a Game Face

3.  How to Think with Pitchers

4.  How to Handle Failure

5.  Mental to Practical: A Typical Trip to the Plate

6.  Long-Term Dedication and Goals

*Marv*.  *Tell us about any fellow players or coaches who helped you with your mental game.*

**Dusty**.  Fellow players—in particular, Orlando Cepeda, Hank Aaron, and Davey Johnson—helped me in terms of setting up the pitcher. I learned to play a cat-and-mouse game with the pitcher. Sometimes I let him think he was in control. Other times I would bluff and pretend that I was in control even when I was not.

*Marv*.  *Were you close enough to any opposing players to receive help with your mental game?*

**Dusty**.  I got a lot of help on my mental game from guys like Billy Williams, Cleon Jones, Willie Stargell, and Tony Perez, who were all on opposing teams.

*Marv*.  *Did anyone help you with two-strike hitting?*

**Dusty**.  Ron Fairly is the guy who taught me how to hit with two strikes and what to think about. All these guys used to talk a lot. Opposing hitters would go out after the game and talk about a pitcher—what he's doing and what to look for—and discuss his tendencies and patterns.

Once when I was 19 years old with the Braves in spring training, I was supposed to go out with the opposing players one night, but Orlando Cepeda wouldn't let me go. He told me to go home and read Norman Vincent Peale's *The Power of Positive Thinking*. That book is what really helped make positive thinking a part of my game.

T here is so much to be said about the mental preparation of a hitter that an entire book could be written on the subject. This chapter will focus on certain topics that are keys to a hitter improving his mental game. Much of what is covered applies to the advanced hitter, but many points pertain to hitters of any age.

Most experienced baseball people will say that hitting is 50–70 percent mental, but for young players, it can be 80–90 percent mental, depending on the physical ability of the player. What's the difference between the minds of younger players and major leaguers when their team scores no runs and has only 4 or 5 hits in two games and then comes back to score 28 runs on 32 hits in the next two games? Certainly there are variables that can cause such a wide swing in results, the primary one being pitching. Often, however, the pitching was not that much different. There must have been some intangible element that prevented the players from doing well in the first two games and a different one that allowed them to do very well in the next two games. If players and coaches could only recognize and define those intangible elements, they could be more in control of the outcome of games!

Success in hitting is contagious, and unfortunately so is failure. That is why, although it may not seem logical, it is much easier to hit successfully after the preceding two or three batters have already gotten base hits than to do so if they have struck out or popped up. *Hitting is a frame of mind*, one that is created by the way the hitter "feels," or "perceives," opportunities at the plate.

The six key aspects of the mental part of hitting are the following.

1. *Physical–mental preparation before game day*. What can the hitter do physically before game day to get himself mentally prepared for success?

2. *Putting on a game face*. How does the hitter feel? What can he do mentally to prepare for today's game?

3. *How to think with pitchers*. How does the hitter learn to think with pitchers, both before and during a time at bat?

4. *How to handle failure*. How does the hitter stay mentally tough when he has failed at the plate on 70 percent of his appearances?

5. *Mental to practical: a typical trip to the plate*. How does the hitter translate his mental preparation to an actual trip to the plate?

6. *Long-term dedication and goals*. What are the hitter's long-term goals and how does he prepare mentally for and stay focused on them?

## 1. Physical–Mental Preparation Before Game Day

Baseball, like nearly any other undertaking in life, involves a great deal of preparation before game day in order to be successful. Baseball can be compared with an algebra class. If a student takes algebra and doesn't do the homework or go to class, then that student hasn't given himself an opportunity to learn. How well can he expect to do on an algebra test? The answer is clear. By the same argument, if a hitter doesn't do the physical–mental practice for baseball and doesn't use his mind to help himself make corrections and reinforce a positive hitting attitude, then how can he expect to be successful at game time?

While most would think it absurd to approach an algebra course without going to class or doing the homework, many hitters approach a baseball game without any physical or mental practice time, and without ever thinking about or working on those aspects of the game that will help them to be successful. A lack of mental preparation is a bad habit that the hitter must avoid if he wants to be successful.

If the player "practices," whether it be algebra or baseball, he is more confident and in control on test or game day. Indeed, "practice" enriches and "exercises" mental attitude. The more a player practices, the more he strengthens his mental attitude, thus controlling his success. Physical preparation has a direct effect on mental preparation. Therefore, a daily practice routine of 50–150 cuts goes a long way to preparing the hitter's mind.

There are those who would argue that practice time has absolutely nothing to do with mental preparation. Nothing is further from the truth. If the hitter experiences success in any form, whether practice or games, his attitude and approach toward competing in games will be much, much better. The difference between an 0 for 20 streak and a 10 for 20 streak is the first base hit. Once a hitter breaks a

bad streak by getting that first hit, it is easier to get the second hit, the third hit, and so on.

As a coach (or parent), what can you do to help your players (or your child) prepare to play? Much of being a coach is how you teach what you know. Thus *how* you communicate with your players is just as important as *what* you communicate. In some ways, you almost have to be able to analyze what the hitter is thinking. Is he up or is he down? Does he need encouragement right now or can he take some constructive criticism? Once you know your players well enough to make such an analysis, you will get a lot more out of them. You can sway players positively just by saying the right things at the right time. Thus, whatever happens before game day to make the hitter feel good about himself, whether it comes from the coach or from the hitter working individually on his own stroke, will only enhance the positive mental feeling he needs to be prepared.

As we mentioned in Chapter 1, regardless of how negative you may be with a player, always end with something positive. Do not leave him walking away with his head down. His level of success is directly proportional to the way he feels about himself.

## 2. Putting on a Game Face

What can a player do to prepare mentally on game day? First, he can be physically prepared. This will support his mental preparation. Thus he must be sure to take pregame batting practice. Each hitter should determine his own comfortable batting practice routine. Some hitters like to take 10 cuts before a game, while some take 50. The important point is to find a routine and stay with it.

Batting practice before game day and on game day place the hitter in a better mental position for that first at bat. A hit on the first at bat relieves a great deal of pressure from the rest of the day. Then the player can just calmly proceed with the remainder of the game. Even if he doesn't get any more hits, the game is still not a total loss.

What else can the hitter do to prepare mentally for game day? Should he do anything special? Should he spend a few minutes alone before game time thinking about what he is going to do?

Does he think about the pitcher? Is he the happy-go-lucky type who passively approaches one game the same as any other? In truth, these all can work, depending on the player. Most successful hitters, however, spend time thinking about the game and about the pitcher.

There is one critical point for players to remember regarding game preparation: A hitter is not preparing himself properly before game time by sitting in the stands talking to his friends. High school players, especially, have a tendency to leave the dugout to go chat with friends. Do not allow such behavior. It is important that players remain focused, not only during but also before the game. After the game is the time to socialize, not before or during.

Although each player prepares differently, many players have superstitions, traditions, or habits on game day. Jeff Mercer, as a player, liked to listen to music before the game. This helped him focus on the game and create a proper mental attitude. Dusty Baker, as a player, liked to eat at a specific time before a game. If he knew the pitcher, he liked to spend time thinking about the kinds of pitches that might be thrown. He also used music to help him visualize the upcoming game. Wade Boggs of the Boston Red Sox likes to eat chicken before every game as part of his mental preparation. Such habits are all part of a player's mental makeup.

Baseball players, traditionally, are very superstitious. Some, like Dusty Baker, do not step on the chalk lines or on third base when running onto the field. In truth, such superstitions would seem to have no bearing on the outcome of the game, but if they help the hitter prepare mentally and get in a routine, then he should not be discouraged in any way from following them.

A hitter needs to be relaxed and confident, with his mind in control. His head must be clear and cool in order to control the burning desire in his heart to succeed. It is normal to be nervous, but he should not be scared. If he is, the pitcher will have a clear advantage from the start.

As a coach, you must be able to read your team on game day and react accordingly. Are the players up or down? How do you adjust your pre-game discussion? Some days your discussion may have nothing to do with the game. It might be about some other sporting event held in town or about a new restaurant. Such seemingly idle chatter can actually allow you to gauge how the players feel and have prepared. It may also help to calm the team down because it will show that you are relaxed about the game. Sometimes it is more important to focus on your own team rather than the opposition.

"A hitter needs to be relaxed and confident, with his mind in control. His head must be clear and cool in order to control the burning desire in his heart to succeed."

At times you might decide to give your team a stern pep talk. Other days you might want to keep everything on a light, humorous level. If you are an experienced coach, you have probably been through many such situations. It is imperative that you keep your finger on the pulse of the team. If the players are ready to go, about all you can do is stand back and let them play, using their skills and doing their best to win. If they are not ready to play, you may need to interject something to help improve their attitude in order to win. This mental preparation is as much your responsibility as making up the lineup card. You need to find a routine that works best for you. Allow yourself some individualism here.

## 3. How to Think with Pitchers

Notice that the title is not "How to Guess with Pitchers." For a hitter, guessing can be an extremely dangerous tactic—one that is better not to adopt unless the hitter is way ahead in the count or is having a really good day and knows his guessing will be correct. It is important, however, to know how to *think* with pitchers— how they pitch, what they are going to throw, what they might do to tip off a particular pitch. In addition, the hitter might try to determine if the pitcher has a throwing pattern.

The hitter can begin to think with the pitcher before ever going to the plate. This is done by making wise use of time in the dugout and in the on-deck circle. For example, he can think about the following.

1. Watch the pitcher when he is warming up. Is he getting breaking balls over the plate? How fast does his fastball seem? Are other kinds of pitches being thrown and is he getting them over the plate? Are his breaking balls in the dirt? Are his fastballs high? The possibilities are endless.

2. Watch the release point of the pitcher. Is it in the same place? Is it low or high? Is it in a different place on a curveball than on a fastball?

3. Watch for signs of the pitcher's fear or frustration, while being careful not to show your own.

Often hitters who bat third, fourth, fifth, or lower in the lineup arrive at the plate with no more idea what the pitcher has been throwing than they did before the game began. It is inexcusable not to insist that hitters pay attention to the pitcher.

A hitter can spot many things while watching the pitcher working against teammates who precede him in the batting order. Following are examples.

1. What has been the first pitch to every batter? Many pitchers tend to throw a fastball on the first pitch. If the hitter knows a fastball is coming and gets it, why not swing at it? It may be the best pitch he gets in that at bat. The pitcher may also change his motion on a curveball, a changeup, or even a fastball.

2. What other pitches did the pitcher throw to the leadoff batter?

3. Is the pitcher throwing harder than normal? If so, rather than trying to swing harder to compensate, the hitter should be sure to get the head of the bat on the ball. The velocity of the pitch will provide the power.

4. Is the pitcher's grip different on a curveball than on a fastball? Is the release point on a curveball different from the release point on a fastball? Is there a difference in arm angle? Is there a difference in the position of the pitcher's hand in the glove?

5. Is the pitcher predictable in the way he shakes off the catcher? For example, he may shake off the catcher every time he wants to throw a curveball, particularly when he is ahead in the count.

6. Is the catcher predictable? Does he signal the pitcher to throw mostly fastballs? What kind of pitch does the catcher signal for when a runner is on first base? When a runner is on third base, does the catcher avoid signaling for the curveball so he won't have to risk catching the pitch in the dirt?

The answers to all these questions can provide definite advantages that the hitter can pick up before ever walking to the plate. But all involve mental preparation!

Knowing what a pitcher is going to throw is often a simple prediction. If the pitcher gets ahead in the count, he may often throw an off-speed pitch. At age 12 or 13, the pitcher might be able to throw a curveball or might try to locate a fastball high and inside in this situation. When a pitcher gets behind in the count at, say, 1–0, 2–0, or 3–1, he will generally throw a fastball. If the batter knows about what to look for, he can then concentrate to make sure he gets a good pitch. This does not mean, however, that the batter should have already made up his mind to swing.

Some pitchers may not like to throw certain pitches or they may like to throw certain pitches in certain spots. There may be a pitcher in your league who throws all fastballs. Most fastball pitchers throw the ball up in the zone. The hitter should then expect the pitch in that location. (A strictly fastball pitcher must be able to throw very hard!) There may be other pitchers who throw all curves. If so, the hitter adapts by concentrating on the lower part of the strike zone. Even that type of pitcher can still be hit, if the batter is patient enough.

Charting pitches (generally done at the high school or college level) can be a great help in picking up on those tendencies of opposing pitchers. This is often done by an assistant coach, but a pitcher who is not playing that day can also serve in this role. The charter keeps track of what the pitcher throws to each of the different hitters, when the hitters made contact, and what kind of pitch was thrown on what count. He also charts such factors as pitch count, location, and variety of pitches. Although such information is not a guarantee, it is still a useful barometer of what the pitcher might be throwing next. By the second or third inning, the team then has a good feel for what the first pitch will be to each hitter. In the major leagues, the pitcher who will throw the following day generally charts his own team's pitcher in order to prepare for the next game.

If, in a certain spot, you feel that the hitter would have an advantage by knowing what you think the pitcher will throw, tell him. Suppose the sixth hitter of the game comes to the plate and the bases are loaded with no outs. If you know the pitcher has thrown five first-pitch fastballs in a row, you should tell the hitter that he will probably be thrown a fastball. He should make sure that it is a good pitch and then hit it hard. Since pitchers have enough advantages to begin with, anything the coach can do to help his team gain the edge will be of great benefit.

To be a good hitter, it helps to think like a pitcher as well. The two share a great deal, although one has a bat and the other a ball. In particular, each wants to control the plate. A good hitter generally has control of at least half the plate, so he must concentrate on controlling the other half. If a batter is good at hitting pitches over the inside part of the plate, then he must work on gaining control of the outside of the plate. Add the two halves together and the batter gains control of the entire plate.

One closing tip is in order regarding a batter's thinking at the plate. Suppose the pitcher has two pitches. Then the hitter has a one-half probability of getting a certain pitch. If the pitcher has three pitches, then the hitter has a one-third probability of getting a certain pitch. Suppose further in the latter situation that the hitter guesses a particular pitch—say, a fastball on the first pitch. If the pitcher throws a curve, then what does the hitter think about on the next pitch? By thinking fastball again, the hitter increases his odds of guessing the pitch simply because a pitcher tends to change his pitches. Many hitters, however, think differently. For example, if the first pitch was a curve, but the hitter guessed a fastball, he may guess something else on the next pitch. He has thereby lowered his odds to one third again, instead of the one-half odds he

would have had by eliminating the curve and assuming the fastball. This is just one example of the mental game within the game that the pitcher and the batter go through. More will be said about this in Chapter 9.

# 4. How to Handle Failure

Failure is a way of life in baseball. Even the highest-paid athletes at the major league level will not get a hit seven out of ten times at bat. How a player deals with failure has a direct impact on his level of success. Often young hitters with a lot of ability expect too much of themselves. When they fail, it adversely affects their performance on the next three, four, or five swings.

The failure factor can be attributed partially to the many advantages that a pitcher has over a batter:

1. The pitcher is standing on a hill above the hitter.
2. The pitcher has a catcher standing behind the plate signaling a predetermined target.
3. The pitcher and the catcher know what kind of pitch is to be thrown.

> A hitter who swings at a good pitch and hits the ball hard *has not failed*!

**4.** The pitcher has seven teammates standing behind him ready to get the ball, even if it has been hit properly.

Amid all of this, the hitter should strive to be sure the pitcher never sees him perspire or look worried. He must always appear to be in control.

A coach can't expect a hitter to feel good about popping up, striking out, or hitting into a double play with the bases loaded and one out. What you can expect him to do, however, is to be levelheaded enough to bounce back from a mistake or an out and not allow failure to drag him down even further. It is important to teach your players that getting angry at themselves can only create more problems. A basketball player can't carry a missed layup back on defense or on to the next shot. Similarly, a baseball player must learn to move from one negative act to the next possible positive act. You will know that a hitter has turned the corner when he can bounce back after every swing.

Suppose the hitter strikes out his first two trips to the plate. If you were to ask him how his day has gone so far, the typical answer would be "not good." What would happen if on his next two at bats he hit the ball out of the ballpark, with the second home run winning the game in the bottom of the last inning? If you then asked him how his day went, his answer would probably be "awesome"! What began as a very poor day ended up a very good day. In all likelihood, a positive mental approach after the first at bat was a contributing factor. In other words, after a failure at the first at bat, why not approach any subsequent at bat with the assumption that it will be successful?

The hitter should not create more failure by the attitude he projects. *He must be careful not to compound one mistake by making another*! This is very difficult for young hitters to understand. Point out to them that most major leaguers take it all in stride. Although they never feel good about failure, they recognize that pitchers quite often do their job well and the hitters are going to make outs. They know

> The hitter should concentrate more on his positive at bats and less on the poor ones. Try to remember feelings and thoughts during positive at bats and build on them!

they are going to strike out sometimes. They know they are going to pop up occasionally, but they do not let it drag them down, because they realize that their team still needs them to come through. A good positive mental attitude will help the team much more than throwing a helmet and batting glove and letting the next at bat be affected by the last one.

The player should also consider the effect that his mental attitude has on his teammates. Throwing his bat, helmet, and batting glove after every out is not a positive reinforcement for the other eight players. In fact, such negative behavior wastes physical and mental energy that might be needed later in the game. Indeed, we have found that it generally takes more effort to be negative than to be positive.

Suppose, on the other hand, that the hitter takes an out in stride and goes on to do an effective job defensively. Suppose he also tries to pick the other players up when they make a mistake and gets a base hit at his next at bat. Such positive behavior is just as contagious as failure. A hitter has the power to select his own attitude. Much of that attitude relates directly to how the hitter feels and how he projects himself to the rest of the team.

One word of caution is in order with regard to handling failure. Suppose the hitter has gone through most of the season and done very well offensively. But then for a week or maybe even two weeks he does not hit the ball well. It is important that he avoid the tendency to make major changes in stance, stride, or other aspects of his swing. The difference between a foul ball and a home run is only about half an inch on the bat. So why make a wholesale change when the bat was off target by only half an inch—certainly a normal human error?

Instead, the hitter should maintain what created that level of success in the beginning. He might consider working harder, maybe getting in some additional swings or having someone watch his swing or perhaps checking a videotape of earlier posi-

"A lot of Dusty's teaching is about the mental aspect of the game—not so much on the physical mechanics of your swing. A lot of baseball is mental. It's almost like everybody in the majors has a good swing. Sometimes it turns into a terrible swing, but the reason is not because of mechanics. The reason is mental. Maybe you play a three-game series against a team that pitches you inside a lot. Then you jump on a plane and go to the next city and the new team pitches you completely different, but you still have it fresh in your mind that the last team pitched you inside, so you try and pull the ball.

"Dusty breaks the mental game down with each individual. He makes you get into your mind and think about what you are doing. He works very hard at his job and gains satisfaction in that. He doesn't come across as wanting you to think he is inspirational—he's just Dusty! He's very good at what he does, but it is a tough job. In the minds of the public, if we hit, it's us, but if we don't hit, it's Dusty. He takes the heat for us."

Matt Williams, San Francisco Giants

tive at bats against recent at bats. Analyzing possible *small* changes may explain why he is not realizing success. Maybe the hitter is somewhat out of rhythm. Maybe he is not using his hips well enough. Maybe his top hand is a bit lazy. No matter what, he should stay away from making radical changes!

> Remember, the hitter bats only one pitch, one at bat, and one game at a time!

The hitter can also make the mistake of overanalyzing. Most of the time a hitting mistake is something simple or perhaps nothing more than just not hitting. Again, remember the hitter is trying to hit that small object (the ball) with another small object (the bat).

The difference between being in a slump—or unfortunate period, as we prefer to say—and being out is in many cases one hit. That one hit might be a bunt. In the scorebook, a bunt single is the same as a line-drive single. All it took was that one hit to pull the hitter out of the slump. If he is hitting the ball hard and the balls are caught, that's unfortunate, but it is no reason for a player to be down on his hitting skills.

Try some short-term goals. For example, a hitter might begin with a goal of getting at least one hit each day. Then after one hit, he can try for two, three, and so on. Anything above and beyond that one hit becomes a bonus. Most younger hitters are at bat an average of three or four times per game. If the hitter goes 1 for 3, he's batting .333 for the year, a very respectable average. If he goes 1 for 4 or 0 for 4 occasionally, it may pull his average down a bit, but anytime the player can hit above .300, he knows that he has done a good job of hitting for that game and for that particular season. He will feel much better trying to salvage the day by fighting for a hit on the final at bat and going 1 for 4, than going 1 for 1 and then mentally letting up to 0 for 3. The result seems to be the same 1 for 4, but that 1 for 1 on the first at bat could have turned into a perfect 4 for 4 day.

## 5. Mental to Practical: A Typical Trip to the Plate

Let's take a mental trip through the hitter's mind on a typical time at bat. At the plate, the hitter should think about the following before the umpire's signal to resume play.

**a)** *Balance:* Get balanced in the batter's box.

**b)** *Relax:* Use breathing to help your state of mind. Inhale and exhale deeply to get extra oxygen in the bloodstream to keep a clear head.

**c)** *Concentrate:* Prepare to concentrate solely on the pitch, allowing no distractions from the opposition or the stands. Create "tunnel vision" toward the pitch.

**d)** *Attack the ball:* Keep only the thought in mind to attack the ball and hit it hard.

When the hitter steps up to the plate, he should not be worried about fundamentals. If the hitter is not prepared fundamentally to hit, then he will probably not be successful. It is your job as a coach to make sure that fundamentals have been taken care of before game time. Stress that each of your players try to do the following when at the plate.

1. *Get a good pitch.* Swing at a pitch in the strike zone that you feel you have a good chance of hitting. You may, for example, prefer a medium high inside pitch.

2. *Attack the ball.* Take a good swing or at least the best swing that you can possibly take, and hit the ball hard.

---

"Dusty helped me with my mental game to the point where I was visualizing what I would do before I would get to the plate. I would already know what I was going to do with the ball. If I feel like I am going to hit a home run, I know it's going to happen. That's the way he taught me to be mentally."

Kevin Mitchell, Seattle Mariners

3. *Try to get deep in the count on the first at bat*, unless runners are in scoring position. You want to see as many pitches as possible, so

you should not be fooled in future at bats by a pitch you have not seen. There is a delicate balance here. Aggressiveness is to be encouraged since you may get only one good pitch to swing at. On the other hand, making good judgments can get you deep in the count on the first at bat.

4. You have four at bats and should not lose one because you are not ready or feeling rushed.

# 6. Long-Term Dedication and Goals

The player and his coaches should make frequent evaluations of his performance. These help to reveal weaknesses so that work can be directed toward improvement. It is imperative for a player and a team to set goals that are high but realistic. Encourage a player to actually write down his goals. They might be as simple as keeping strike-outs to no more than 5. Other goals might be to hit .400, to get 3 more walks than strike-outs, to get 40 RBIs, to get 5 game-winning hits, or to achieve a 1-to-10 ratio of strike-outs to at bats. Another goal might be to make it to the major leagues. Whatever the goals, have your players write them down and put them where they can be seen every day. After a while, those goals will become almost an obsession.

The odds of making the major leagues are small. Only a very few individuals ever reach that level. However, there is a great deal that a player can gain from setting goals and attempting to attain them. The character traits that a player develops in working toward success in baseball will be invaluable in whatever he does in life.

Whatever the player undertakes in baseball or in life, he should set his goals high but reachable. New goals should not be established until the first one has been reached or the chance to reach it has passed. Above all, each player should be encouraged to give his best effort at all times.

# Six Key Aspects of the Mental Part of Hitting

1. Physical–mental preparation before game day
   - Acquire good practice habits regarding hitting.

2. Putting on a game face
   - Acquire a routine.
   - Be relaxed and confident.

3. How to think with pitchers
   - Observe the pitcher warming up and during the game.
   - Watch the release point(s) of the pitcher.
   - Watch the pitcher throwing to other hitters.

4. How to handle failure
   - Try to bounce back after every negative experience.
   - In an unfortunate period, do not react by making drastic changes in batting style.

5. Mental to practical: a typical trip to the plate
   - When at the plate, think about the following before the umpire's signal to resume play: balance, relaxation, concentration, and attacking the ball.
   - On a trip to the plate, get a good pitch and attack the ball. Try to get deep in the count on the first at bat, unless runners are in scoring position, and don't get in the batter's box until ready.

6. Long-term dedication and goals
   - Set goals and work toward them.
   - Don't change goals until the first one is reached.

## Quick Tips

- The hitter should concentrate on his positive at-bats rather than on the poor ones. Try to remember feelings and thoughts during those positive at bats and build on them!

- A hitter who swings at a good pitch and hits the ball hard *has not failed*!

- The hitter bats only one pitch, one at bat, and one game at a time!

# CHAPTER NINE

# The Advanced Hitter

1. Extrapolating on the Systematic Approach to Hitting
2. The Mental–Physical Combination
3. Being Natural
4. Enhancing Concentration
5. Using the Opposite Field
6. Two-Strike Hitting
7. Power Hitting
8. Hitting Special Pitches
9. Setting Up the Pitcher
10. Gardening at the Plate
11. Fungos, Pepper, and Music
12. Hitting Clues from the Defense
13. Hitting to the Opposite Field
14. Knowing the Opposition's Philosophy
15. Knowing the Umpires
16. Varying Bat Sizes and Stances
17. The Hitter's Triangle
18. Spring Training
19. Bat Vibrations and Sweet Spots
Conclusion

**Marv.** *Can you tell us what it is like to coach professional hitters?*

**Dusty.** Coaching a professional hitter is more difficult sometimes than coaching an amateur hitter because obviously the professional has already had a tremendous amount of success or he wouldn't be there in the first place. You would be surprised, though, at how open to suggestions the professional hitter is, especially if he's not doing well.

**Marv.** *What is the hardest part of working with a professional hitter?*

**Dusty.** The most difficult time is helping him when he is not doing well. Almost every professional player was the best at some time in his career. Now he's with the best of the best and if he isn't fundamentally sound and has been surviving on natural ability alone, flaws in fundamentals will show up and the hitter will become frustrated. He might reach a limit simply because of a lack of concentration or a flaw in any fundamental we've talked about earlier in the book. If the opposition finds a weakness, they will obviously use it to exploit the hitter. Then the hitter becomes so conscious of this weakness that he loses the strong part of his game.

In the professional game, coaching a hitter is so complicated now with film, video tapes, scouting reports, and charts, that a hitter must constantly adjust to what the opposition is doing. He can no longer assume that he can just go out there and do well every day on ability alone. Every game becomes a constant adjustment, sometimes from one at bat to the next, especially when the opposition changes pitchers all the time.

**Marv.** *What is your approach to dealing with the professional hitter?*

**Dusty.** The professional hitter is a lot like a high-priced thoroughbred horse in that you're dealing with a big ego inside a young body. It's similar to dealing with a young man in a man's body.

**Marv.** *Were you like a thoroughbred as a player?*

**Dusty.** Yes, only in today's game it's getting tougher. With the overall pressure to win, the team management's patience is shorter. Teams want to win today. They don't want to rebuild and wait until tomorrow anymore. A hitting coach is often in a fast teaching situation where he has to nearly force-feed information and hope it sinks in and is correct. The luxury of time to let a hitter evolve and develop at his own pace is no more.

This chapter focuses on the advanced hitter who is pursuing a college career or is already in the professional ranks. The reader may come to this chapter with varying goals. He might be young and want to see what is ahead. He might be interested only in certain topics, say, hitting curveballs or hitting for power. He may be a coach looking for ideas. Thus the reader can choose topics according to his own needs.

## 1. Extrapolating on the Systematic Approach to Hitting

*A Definition of Hitting.* Just what is hitting to an advanced hitter? The following is a rigorous definition: *Hitting* is defined as leading with the knob of the bat, staying inside the baseball at the proper bat angle, and getting the head of the bat to the ball with the hitter's head down on the ball.

The bottom hand is to be dominant. It maximizes the hitter's chances of getting the head of the bat to the ball with the head down. It also pulls the bat by leading the knob at the ball, staying inside the baseball, across, and out through the zone. The top hand then finishes the swing.

> "Hitting is defined as leading with the knob of the bat, staying inside the baseball at the proper bat angle, and getting the head of the bat to the ball with the hitter's head down on the ball."

*The Power V.* When the bat is brought into the strike zone and is at the moment of impact, the palm of the player's top hand should face up. The bat is then in what is called a hammer position (see Figures 1a and 1b), which is a strong impact position. Indeed, if someone tried to resist the hitter's swing at this point, the hitter would find that he is strongest when the palm of the top hand faces up, and weaker when the wrist is in other curved positions. He has not allowed the hands to roll over. The bat continues through its contact with the ball,

and the arms and shoulders extend to form what is called a **Power V**. The head of the hitter is between the V. A correct Power V is shown in Figure 1(c), and an incorrect one is shown in Figure 1(d). Note that the arms are twisted and curled. Very little power has been imparted to the ball.

The hitter moves from the hammer position to the Power V in an instant. The full extension into the Power V does not occur until *during or after* the ball has been hit. After the Power V, the hands are allowed to roll over and the follow-through is completed. No matter where the pitch is—inside, outside, or across the plate—the goal of the hitter is a Power V.

On the inside pitch, the hitter brings his hands down and across his body. The hitter need not achieve complete extension on this pitch to get maximum power because such a pitch is usually pulled down a line where the distance to the fence may be 330 feet rather than 400 feet to straight centerfield. Since most inside pitches are fastballs, the hitter just wants to get to the ball and hit it fair. Thus he must use his bottom arm to pull down and across the zone in order to keep the ball fair.

**FIGURE 1**

Note the palm is pointed upward at impact.

The hammer position

**A. The impact position of the bat on the ball.**

**B. The hammer position.**

A correct Power V

An incorrect Power V

**C. A correct Power V.**

**D. An incorrect Power V.**

***Step to Swing.*** A part of the systematic approach that can be expanded is the end of the stride and the beginning of the swing. Recall that at the end of the stride the hitter places his front toe down gently as if landing on thin ice. The front heel then goes down, signaling the start of the swing. These two ideas can be combined to say that the hitter should **step to swing**. Many professional hitters erroneously step *and* swing at the same time. However, he shouldn't step *and* swing; he steps *to* swing. The difference is subtle but important. Whereas step *and* swing occur at the same time, there are two distinct stages in step *to* swing (see Figure 2).

**"The hitter doesn't step *and* swing;**

**he steps *to* swing."**

***Hitting Against a Firm Front Side.*** Hitting is best achieved against, but not over, the front side. While the hitter is *against* the firm front side, his upper body stays over the ball. Hank Aaron achieved this better than any

Place toe down gently as if stepping on thin ice.

Heel goes down, signaling start of swing.

**FIGURE 2**
*Step to swing.*

*Hank Aaron hitting against a firm front side.*

National Baseball Library, Cooperstown, N.Y.

other player. He stayed over the ball with his upper body and kept his body in and over the plate after completing the swing.

Often hitters fall back off the ball, releasing the front shoulder. If the hitter stays over the ball, he will not pull off the ball and thus he will see the ball longer. Therefore, he should keep the upper part of his body over the ball, always looking down at the ball (see Figure 3). If he can't see the top of the ball, the odds are it is too high anyway.

*Weight Transfer and Follow-Through.* The hitter achieves weight transfer in the swing by stepping to swing and hitting against a firm front side. His weight transfer begins by moving backward in the inward turn and then shifting against the front side. When the hitter rolls up on his back foot, his weight is now on his back toe but braced against the front side (see Figure 4).

The arms and the hands of the hitter serve mainly to transfer the energy of the body's rotation. The follow-through is designed to *ensure* correct movements before the ball is hit. The hitter's goal is to accelerate the bat

**FIGURE 3**

Hitting off a firm front side →

Incorrect: the front side is bent.

*A. Hitting correctly off a firm front side.*     *B. Hitting incorrectly off a firm front side.*

**FIGURE 4**
*Weight transfer.*

*A. Beginning stance.*

*B. The weight transfer begins by moving backward in the inward turn.*

*C. It then shifts against the front side when the hitter rolls up on his back foot.*

through the zone, which ensures the follow-through. If the hitter doesn't follow through, he is decelerating. The advanced hitter starts slow and short, accelerates to the ball (especially the last 6–12 inches prior to contact), and then finishes long. This creates a dynamic pop on the ball from the bat through the zone and a long finish.

*Hitting Flyballs and Ground Balls.* Flyballs and pop-ups generally occur when the hitter is late in the swing. Flyballs can also occur when a hitter is uppercutting too much, falling back from the ball, or not staying over the ball.

Ground balls occur when the hitter is early in his swing or has a quick front shoulder, causing him to open prematurely. Then in order to hit the ball, he must swing down and back up in an "∽"-shaped curve and roll over to hit the ball. The changeup is a special situation. If the hitter is early on a changeup, he is apt to hit a flyball.

*Swinging with One Hand.* Using both hands is preferable whenever possible in hitting. However, a hitter might let the top hand go and swing with one hand if he gets to the ball early. This can happen either when the hitter makes an error timing a pitch or when the pitcher throws a changeup. He then can slow his swing down by removing his top hand. This should be done when the ball is well away from the hitter, because he has more extension with one hand than he does with two hands. It can also be done if a batter has a problem not following through on his swing. It should *only* be done, however, *after* contact has been made. By letting one hand go, the hitter can slow down his swing and hit the ball back through the middle.

"The hitter should use two hands through contact with the ball. He can let the top hand go once he gets full extension and the ball is already gone."

If the hitter doesn't take one hand off the bat when he is too early, he will end up rolling his wrists over waiting for the ball, then hitting a ground ball to the shortstop if he's a right-handed

hitter or a ground ball to second base if he's a left-handed hitter. The hitter should use two hands through contact on the ball. Then the hitter can let the top hand go once he gets full extension and the ball is already gone.

## 2. The Mental–Physical Combination

Spending time on the mental–physical combination nearly always results in enhanced playing skills. The key to unlocking this part of a player's skills is physical training, especially for the professional hitter. This training should begin in the off-season. Any ballplayer will tell you that there are always certain games during the season when he just does not feel like playing. He may be mentally tired or physically tired or some combination of both. This feeling toward physical conditioning occurs during the off-season as well.

Larry Doby, a former Cleveland Indian, once said that a player gets ready during the off-season for the long marathon race that he will run during the actual season. He is getting his body physically ready for the long

haul, and, just as important, he is also getting his mind prepared for the days when he doesn't feel like playing. This training will only enhance his performance during the regular season.

Almost every player will be injured at some point during the course of the season. The better the shape he is in, however, the quicker he will heal. In turn, the quicker players heal, the more often the team will have its front-line players on the field, thus increasing the team's probability of winning. Since the key is to remain on the active list as much as possible, a player's physical therapy with the team's trainers is very, very important. If a player is injured, he must get to the clubhouse early and stay late after the game.

A team's second-line players must be in as good, or sometimes better, shape as the front-line players. During the course of the season, front-line players need to conserve their physical energy for the actual playing of the game. Thus they cannot spend as much time on physical training. A second-line player, however, must be ready to enter the game on a moment's notice. He cannot afford to go in out of shape, thus increasing his chances for a pulled muscle or other injury and losing his opportunity to help the team and advance his own career.

We cannot overemphasize the importance of off-season conditioning—mental conditioning as well as physical conditioning. Physical training helps a player feel better about himself mentally. When he is physically prepared, he is mentally prepared as well. He knows his body is ready, and he visualizes himself doing well.

Nowadays players have many off-season training aids, such as weight machines. These enhance their physical training during the season as well. Some players who may be in great shape during spring training might get out of shape during the course of the year because they are afraid that if they exert too much energy in conditioning, their playing skills will suffer. It is important, however, that players form the habit of spending time after a game on weight machines or light weight training. Some players have trouble keeping their weight down, while others have trouble keeping their strength up. Light weight training will help them keep their weight down and maintain strength during the season. Home teams usually have

weight-training facilities readily at hand for their players. For the player on the road, unfortunately, such conveniences are often either nonexistent or hard to find.

A player's diet is also very important to his mental–physical conditioning. *When* he eats is almost as critical as *what* he eats. The worst is to be trying to digest a heavy meal just before game time! Hank Aaron made it a practice to eat his major meal around 1:00 P.M or 2:00 P.M. if he had a night game. If he ate beef or something as heavy, he would eat earlier. If he had to eat later, he would choose chicken, fish, or pasta, which are all easier to digest.

Another beneficial routine is to stock up on carbohydrates during the main meal, and then have something light, such as fruit, near game time. Many players eat after a game, but this tactic can be counterproductive if he ends up feeling better physically after the game than he did before the game. The goal is to feel his best *for* the game.

A player should strive to get his body into whatever routine works best for him, teaching it, in a sense, when to be hungry and when not to be hungry. It is very difficult for a player to handle his diet and sleep habits when on the road. Both contribute to his mental and physical makeup. His game has to be at the top of his list of priorities.

*The Game of Ones.* Another way in which a player can fight the mental battle on a day when he doesn't feel like playing is to play a ***game of ones***. That is, he sets as a goal for the game, say, one run scored, one RBI, one hit, or one of something else that is positive. Of course, he wants to finish the day with as many of those "ones" as possible to aid his team. On a daily basis, those "ones" can add up to a great season. In the major leagues, a player is considered to have had a great season if he accounts for 200 runs by himself, whether it's 100 runs or 100 RBI's or some other combination. Keep in mind, though, that those 200 runs come *one at a time.*

The game of ones can be played in other ways. Suppose a player is 0–3, but on his last at bat he gets one hit to put him at 1–4. He will probably feel a lot better than if he had been 1–1 and *then* ended up 1–4. A professional hitter should never give away an at bat

**Marv.** *What do you tell your players in order to help them with their mental–physical conditioning?*

**Dusty.** I always say, "To play the game, you don't have to satisfy anybody but God, your family, and yourself. This helps keep the pressure off. But you have to prepare yourself. It's like tuning your car. You've got to keep your car in tip-top shape. You've got to keep your tires with the proper amount of air in them and with the needed tread on them. They're like your feet. You have to take care of your body because this is your automobile—your vehicle to performance.

simply by not being mentally prepared when he goes into the box. Since he will probably get only four at bats per game, he must make each one count. Each pitch can change the course of the entire at bat. Let's say that on a 1–1 count, he swings at a bad pitch because his concentration wasn't there. Now he's 1–2 instead of 2–1—with one pitch, he has gone from being in the driver's seat to being on the defensive.

A player can also improve his mental game during an unfortunate period (or "slump" as we do not like to call it). Suppose he goes 0–4 for 20 games. He then has a .000 batting average for that period. But suppose he can manage to squeak in one hit in each of those 20 games. Now he is 20–80—it may not sound like much, but it is a .250 batting average. By a little extra effort, he has converted 0–80 to 20–80. Those 20 extra hits would change a batting average of, say, 123/446 = .276 to 143/446 = .321.

*Non-At-Bats.* Walks, sacrifice-fly RBI's, or sacrifice bunts do not count as official at-bats when a batting average is computed. Because they do not cause any change in the average, we can think of them as ***non-at-bats***. They are important, however, in dealing with unfortunate periods. A player can turn a slump into a mini-slump with a couple of non-at-bats. They contribute to his batting average in a sense. Suppose a hitter is hitting .300; then he has a 7 out of 10 chance of making an out. If he's in a slump, however, the odds are probably greater than 7 out of 10 that if he gets that extra at bat, he will make an out. So several non-at-bats may improve his average over the season. Let's say that a player is 1–3 in each of 3 games. That translates to 3–9, or a .333 batting average. If he had gone 1–4 over those same 3 games, his average would be .250. Thus non-at-bats can take a player from a .333 average to .250.

*Not Wasting At Bats.* When a hitter goes to the plate, he wants to get as many hits as he can for as long as he can. Pete Rose was about the greediest hitter who ever played the game. If he got a hit on his first at bat, there was a good chance that he would end up 2–3, 3–4, or 4–4 that night. He always looked for the big total hit count instead of throwing away his last two at bats trying to hit a home run. Suppose a hitter has two hits and throws away his last two at bats by playing around trying to hit a home run. If he ends up 2–4 and then goes 0–4 the next day, he has a .250 batting average. By trying just for a base hit, however, he might be 3–4 on the first day. Then even if he goes 0–4 the next day, he has a .375 average. Thus the hitter should never give away an at bat. He should maximize every opportunity at the plate.

**"One of a hitter's primary enemies is tension. If he can eliminate that physical and mental tension, he will be a much better hitter."**

## 3. Being Natural

So much has been written and discussed about hitting that a player can get caught up in the details and forget to be relaxed and natural at the plate. Certainly the hitter wants to tend to the details that lead to good fundamentals. At some point, though, he has to let his muscle memory take over, put it all together, and just hit.

One of a hitter's primary enemies is tension. To be natural, the hitter should attempt, as much as possible, to eliminate any physical and mental tension. The more tension-free he is,

the more fluid he is. The more fluid he is, the more bat speed he has and the less strain he puts on his eyes.

## 4. Enhancing Concentration

Most people have trouble holding eye concentration on an object over 3 or 4 seconds. To enhance and increase this concentration, the hitter might try the following drill, which can be done at home. Dusty Baker learned this drill from his friend, the late Lyman Bostock. Make a chart like the one shown in Figure 5, which contains a

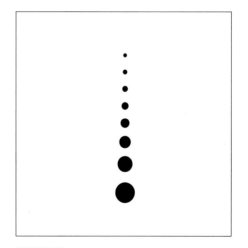

**FIGURE 5**

sequence of solid circular dots of various sizes. Start with the largest dot and stare at it for as long as possible without blinking. Then clear your eyes and repeat the drill with the same dot. Concentrate on the next smaller dot the next day until eventually you are looking at the smallest dot. If you can concentrate on something as minute as that smallest dot, you can definitely concentrate on a baseball, because it will seem even bigger than it normally does. Some players can concentrate better than others, but the one who can concentrate on a daily basis, pitch after pitch, is the one who will give away fewer at bats. Enhanced concentration leads to a higher batting average.

Another weakness in concentration often seen at the advanced level is a tendency to drift forward toward the ball. This means that the hitter is not making the proper inward turn. He doesn't have to go get the ball—it will come to him! With the exception of the low-and-away pitch, which could be a problem if he doesn't have proper plate coverage, every pitch will come across the plate sooner or later.

To enhance his concentration, the hitter has to maintain a cool mind. The epitome of a good hitter is one who has a burning desire to succeed in his heart but a cool enough mind to control those emotions. He must be able to shut out the crowd and the situation by reminding himself that in tough, tight situations the pitcher is the one with the stress. The hitter is not in trouble when the bases are loaded. He will not end up with an L for loss beside his name. Thinking of this will often help release a hitter's tension, especially when he is in a tight situation.

Every at bat is a battle between the hitter and the pitcher. If the pitcher gets the hitter one time, then the hitter will get him the next time. If the pitcher does get him the next time, the hitter will do better the time after that. It's all about a matter of determination and desire and, most of the time, who wants it the most.

Every once in a while there will be a pitcher who is clearly better than the hitter he's facing, but it doesn't occur often at the professional level. Most of the time the final result is simply a matter of determination and desire. The worst thing to see in a hitter is one who gives in and swings at a bad pitch on an 0–2 count rather than fouling off that pitch, fouling off another pitch, concentrating, breathing, fouling off another pitch, and taking a pitch for a ball. In this manner, the count situation could change from 0–2 to 1–2, from 1–2 to 2–2, and then 2–2 to 3–2, leaving the hitter finally in control to get a hit.

# 5. Using the Opposite Field

While not an absolute, most higher batting average hitters tend to be opposite-field hitters. This is not meant to imply that everyone should try to be an opposite-field hitter, but it reveals a possible key to getting back into synchronization, rhythm, and good hitting.

When a player is not hitting well, he is usually not seeing the ball well. A sign that a hitter is doing well is when he hits the ball most often to his pull field. Then the hitter is probably as close to perfect as he can get. When he is struggling and not pulling the ball well, a good tactic is to go to the opposite field and then work his hits back around the outfield to his pull field as he gets back to the desired stroke.

There is less margin for error hitting the ball to the opposite field. The hitter has to wait on his feet a little longer. Most players also have to give up some power if they hit to the opposite field. In the major leagues, there seem to be more hits to the opposite field than there are to the pull field. When the opposition knows that the player is going to hit the ball to the opposite field, it tends to spread out its defense. If the hitter can show the opposition that he can use the whole field, he has more room out there for the ball to fall for a hit. When a hitter consistently pulls the ball, the opposition positions its defense accordingly and thus is more apt to get the hitter out. The hitter may complain that he is unlucky, but in fact he has been victimized by his tendency to pull the ball. If he has a reputation for hitting to the opposite field, he will gain an advantage because the defense will not know where the ball is going.

If a hitter is able to hit to the opposite field, there are other skills in effect. He has more bat control, and he is able to wait longer. He is not apt to be fooled. Most higher-average hitters—players like Rod Carew, George Brett, Wade Boggs, Tony Gwynn, and Willie McGee—tend to be opposite-field hitters. Almost every good hitter, except for such greats as Hank Aaron and Ted Williams, uses the opposite field. Aaron and Williams were unusual, though, because the inside pitch never bothered them; that is, they could not be jammed. Although most pitchers don't throw inside for strikes, the hitter should show the pitcher that he can handle that pitch to keep the pitcher from exploiting such a weakness.

## 6. Two-Strike Hitting

The number-one weakness with professional hitters is that they don't know how to hit with two strikes. A good hitter cannot be afraid to do so, however. The following is a two-strike hitting tactic for an advanced hitter who has good fundamental techniques.

1. He looks for a pitch in his weakest area—say, low and away.
2. He chokes up a bit to attain quickness and bat control.
3. He sets himself to hit the ball up the middle.
4. He tries to hit on the top half of the ball, concentrating on staying over the ball with his upper body. In this manner, he is trying to hit either a line drive or a ground ball up the middle.
5. He stays aggresssive with his swing, not leaving a pitch to the decision of the umpire.
6. He loosens his grip on the bat to attain a quicker, shorter stroke.

*Pete Rose choking up to hit.*

With two strikes, the two-strike hitter actually gets more aggressive. He loosens his hands up so that he can foul off some balls, if necessary. The hitter does not want to hit fair those balls that are too close to take, since he would be taking a chance on the umpire calling a third strike. If he does hit such a ball, it will probably end up being nothing more than a ground ball to the shortstop or second baseman.

Two-strike hitting is a skill that comes with practice and bat control, especially with the low-and-away pitch. The great Manny Mota had that kind of bat control. If he didn't want to hit a particular ball fair, he would just flip the bat at the pitch and foul it either over in the dugout or in the stands for the fans. Brett Butler and Pete Rose are other examples of those who used this tactic.

## 7. Power Hitting

Suppose an advanced hitter is proficient with the fundamentals of hitting; then he can experiment with power hitting and striving for home runs. One way to experiment is to develop a slight upswing. This can be very effective for power hitting, but it is very difficult to perfect without turning it into an uppercut. Most hitters who do have slight upswings also have a tendency to uppercut at times. There is a difference between an upswing and an uppercut. The slight-upswing hitter stays in the hitting zone longer than the uppercut hitter. If the hitter can perfect that slight upswing and stay smooth and rhythmic at the same time, then he probably has the optimal power swing. Ted Williams was truly masterful in his use of a slight upswing.

A proven power hitter, in a situation in which he can win the game with a home run or an extra base hit, should try to think of hitting in a fan-shaped area from left center to right center. How many times does it happen late in a ballgame that a power hitter gets "his" pitch and ends up pulling it foul? Because he doesn't get his pitch very often, he doesn't want to waste it by pulling it foul. If as a right-handed hitter he tries to hit from left center to right center and still happens to be a little early, the ball will go to dead left field, still in the ballpark. Should he be a little late, the ball will go to right field, still in fair territory. Therefore, he will not be too early on most break-

*Ted Williams was a slight upswing hitter.*

National Baseball Library, Cooperstown, N.Y.

keep the player from making the mistake of front shoulder early release. A quick front shoulder or side causes the hitter to give away too much of the outside part of the plate, where pitchers are taught to throw late in the game.

It is common to hear a baseball player comment in an interview that he was the most surprised guy in the ballpark after hitting a home run. A player "sits on a pitch" if he waits for a certain kind of pitch in a particular part of the strike zone. If a hitter is sitting on a pitch, concentrating properly, and not overreacting, then once he gets that pitch, he knows he can hit the ball hard, hopefully for a home run. Many hitters try to lift the ball out of the ballpark. If a hitter has home-run power, however, he shouldn't have to do so. If he does, he will inevitably pop it up. What he wants to do is to drive the ball between left center and right center. If hitting the ball hard doesn't carry it over the fence, then he might at least get an extra base hit and the next batter could drive him in.

The primary goal of a power hitter should be to finish the swing long. Most power hitters should *still* hold

ing balls or off-speed pitches and he will not be late on fastballs. He wants to hit to the big part of the ballpark.

Hitting in a fan-shaped area from left center to right center also tends to

YOU CAN TEACH HITTING

## The power hitter:

1. creates a slight upswing but not an uppercut or a loop in his swing;
2. directs his power swings to the area between left center and right center;
3. does not try to lift the ball;
4. finishes long;
5. waits for the right pitch.

the bat in their fingers. If the player decides to hit the ball to the opposite field, then he could make adjustments with regard to the bottom hand (see Chapter 2, p. 28).

A successful power hitter is careful not to swing at every pitch. He simply waits for the right pitch and to do this, he must be more disciplined and patient. When he gets that pitch, he has to be controlled enough to keep from overswinging and missing. It might be the first pitch or it might be the second pitch. It might even be the last pitch. He can hit only one home run

at a time, but he must be ready for it from the very first pitch.

# 8. Hitting Special Pitches

Probably the greatest challenge for an advanced hitter is developing the ability to hit special pitches such as sliders, curveballs, slurves, sinkers, changeups, screwballs, forkballs, split-finger fastballs, and knuckleballs. Some say that a sinker is the toughest pitch in baseball and the slider is a close second, though this assessment varies among batters. Many factors affect the flight path of a pitched baseball. Among them is the release point of the pitcher—whether it be overhand, three-quarter arm, side arm, or submarine. Another factor is the combination of the seams on the baseball and the way in which the pitcher grips them to create an axis of spin.

Although we cannot cover all the factors, we will spend some time discussing spin and motion to provide some background for hitting special pitches. Any round object that is spin-

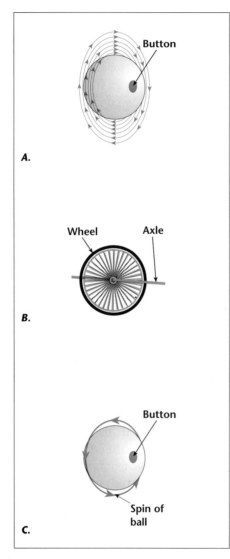

**FIGURE 6**
*Spin and rotation of a round, spinning object.*

ning—in particular, a baseball—looks like the one shown in Figure 6(a). The spin can be compared to a wheel rotating on an axis, as shown in Figure 6(b). The end of an "axis" on a baseball, if it can be seen, appears visually like a spot on the ball that is not spinning. That spot is referred to as a "button" and is represented by the black spot in Figure 6(c). It is like the end of the axle on a wheel. The spin on the ball is shown in the figure by the arrowed arc about its middle. The arc is like the outside of the wheel. One key to understanding the flight path of certain pitches is the location of the button on the ball.

*Fastball.* The typical flight of a *fastball* as thrown by a right-handed pitcher is shown in Figure 7(a). The ball generally follows a straight-line path down from the release point on the pitcher's hand to the catcher. A typical fastball has bottom spin, with the location of the button as shown in Figure 7(b). Though release point can be a factor, the spin of the fastball is frequently end over end with the buttons on the side. Since the buttons are on the side, they cannot be seen by the hitter, even though they are seen somewhat in the drawing because of the added black circles.

The speed of a fastball is affected by the way in which the ball is held on its stitches or seams. A "two-seam" fastball is held with the two top fingers placed on the narrow part of the stitches (see Figure 8a), while the other fingers do not touch any seams. A "four-seam" fastball is held with the two top fingers across one wide seam (see Figure 8b). The bottom fingers also touch seams on the bottom part of the ball.

The seams have many important effects on a baseball as well. First of all, at the speed at which a baseball is thrown, the seams create a turbulence in which the ball goes faster. The same idea works for a golfball, which goes faster because of its dimples. If you were to take the seams off a baseball or the dimples from a golfball, each would go slower, because the air would then be closer to the ball, causing greater friction.

A four-seam fastball exposes more horizontal-seam area to the air than does a two-seam fastball and thus travels 3 or 4 miles per hour faster than a two-seam fastball.* This translates to

*For more details, see Syd Thrift and Barry Shapiro, *The Game According to Syd* (New York: Simon and Schuster, 1990), pp. 31ff.

**FIGURE 7**
*A. The typical flight of a fastball.*

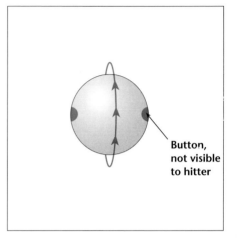

*B. The spin and buttons on a fastball.*

Button, not visible to hitter

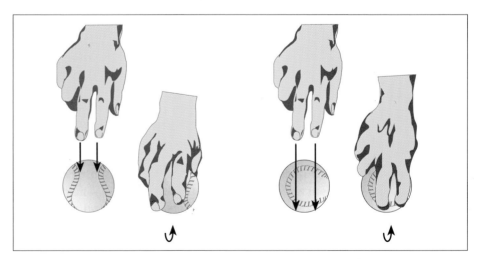

**FIGURE 8**
*A. The two-seam fastball.*          *B. The four-seam fastball.*

about a 30-inch difference in reaction time for the hitter. Outfielders are generally taught to throw four-seam fastballs back to the infield for two reasons. One, the throw comes in faster, and two, it is apt to be more accurate because a two-seam throw tends to tail off more to the left or the right and down.

*Slider.* Figure 9(a) shows the typical flight of a **slider** as thrown by a right-handed pitcher. Note that the pitch looks like a fastball, but it breaks down and away at the last instant. The button on a slider often occurs on the stitching of the ball, and is shown in Figure 9(b). A slider is released off the pitcher's fingers almost as though he were throwing a football spiral. The button on a slider is like the point on the football. Thus the spin of the slider is tilted and the point faces the hitter somewhat, while the button on the other side of the ball faces the pitcher. Clearly the task of seeing the button is a formidable one, perhaps accomplished only by an advanced hitter with exceptional visual skills.

All pitches are designed to look like fastballs. Thus a hitter should anticipate a fastball, but look for anything minutely different, such as in the case

**FIGURE 9**
*A. The flight of a slider.*

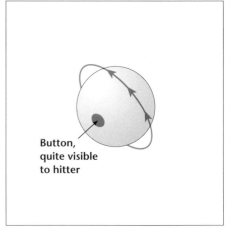

Button, quite visible to hitter

*B. The spin and button on a slider.*

of a slider. It is, of course, a big advantage to know when a slider is coming, and seeing that button is a good clue that a sharp-breaking slider is coming in. The slider looks initially like a fastball, but breaks almost horizontally to the right at the last instant. For this reason, the slider is the second most difficult pitch to hit. The tighter the spin on a slider, the harder it is to pick up and recognize its flight.

With a slider, the hitter must use his imagination to anticipate the flight of the ball. If he picks up the rotation,

then he can hopefully anticipate how far the ball will break. Some major league pitchers (Hall-of-Famer Rollie Fingers and Larry Anderson are examples) can throw 3 or 4 different types of slider, making it especially difficult to pick up the flight of the ball. The ball seems to jump all around because the hitter doesn't know which slider is being thrown. The toughest slider is the one that barely moves—the late breaker. Many hitters return to the dugout shaking their heads over that pitch—a rude awakening to the beginning professional player.

*Curveball.* A **curveball** is thrown off a pitcher's hand with top spin, as shown in Figure 10(a). The buttons on a curveball are somewhat on the side and hard to see. Figure 10(b) shows the spin and buttons on such a curveball.

Many clues to hitting a curveball have been mentioned earlier: the release point, the ball popping up, the way the pitcher holds the ball in his mitt and possibly the way in which he winds up.

Again, as with any other breaking pitch, the player must hit the curveball with imagination. If he swings at the pitch where he first sees it, the only curve he will ever hit is the one that seems to "hang," meaning that it tends to stay up and not curve to any real degree. He must hit a breaking pitch where it's going, using his imagination to anticipate the flight of the ball. When the hitter first sees a curve, it will look like a fastball. (Indeed, as we mentioned earlier, all pitches except a knuckleball are designed to look like a fastball.) The hitter tries to "sit down" to hit the curve, which allows him to stay coiled. Tommy Davis, formerly of the Los Angeles Dodgers, used the term "sit to hit"

**FIGURE 10**
**A. The flight of a curveball.**

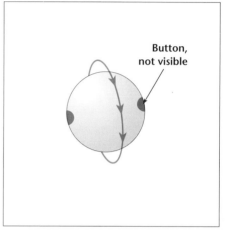

Button, not visible

**B. The spin and buttons on a curveball.**

**FIGURE 11**
*Sit to hit. Note the back knee and hips.*

(see Figure 11). When the pitch comes in, the hitter just uncoils. He must have a delay mechanism in order to let the ball get to him. Then he imagines where the pitch is going and hits it.

An effective hitter tries to swing at high breaking balls and low fastballs. Hitters tend to swing at high fastballs because the pitches are at eye level and they can see them well. Adding to the problem is that at some point, most hitters tag a high fastball and hit it long. But for every one such addictive hit, the batter will pop up 25 others, miss another 25, and foul off still another 25. With those odds, the high pitch is not even worth the risk of a swing, even though most young hitters will swing at it anyway. The advanced hitter needs to think carefully about the difference between a high breaking ball and a high fastball. He should swing at a high breaking ball even though it might be a ball, but *not* at a high fastball in the same location that's a ball. He does not want to have to wait to deal with a low-and-away breaking ball on the black of the plate (outside edge) that is tough to hit. It is easier to hit a breaking ball before it drops.

*Slurve.* A **slurve** can be thought of as a pitch that is somewhere between a curveball and a slider. On a slurve, the hitter will see a button. If he sees it more over the plate, it's a good chance it will be a strike. If it starts out, when it leaves the pitcher's hand, on the outer part of the plate and if the hitter can pick it up breaking, it will be way off the plate by the time it arrives.

*Screwball.* The path of a **screwball** off a right-handed pitcher is very much like the path of a curveball off a left-handed pitcher. Thus it breaks down and in to the right-handed batter and down and away to the left-handed batter. If a pitcher has an effective screwball, he is most likely a left-handed pitcher. Thus, since he faces mostly right-handed hitters, his screwball follows a path like a curveball off a right-handed pitcher. Such a right-handed batter would deal with such a pitch the same way he would a curveball.

*Sinker.* The **sinker** is the toughest pitch in baseball. Its flight is shown in Figure 12(a). Note that off a right-handed pitcher, the sinker looks at first like a fastball, but late in its path it drops down and in to a right-handed batter. Most effective sinkerball pitchers have this pitch as a natural gift; Orel Hershiser, Roger McDowall, Alejandro Pena, and Scott Erickson are examples. Generally the player ends up hitting over the top of the ball, creating a ground ball. The goal of a sinkerball relief pitcher is to come in and get the hitter to hit a ground ball into a double play. Thus he can get the defense out of trouble quicker than any pitcher in baseball.

The button on a sinker is on the side and is not visible (see Figure 12b). The pitch spins somewhat like a screwball but with the button more on the side and thrown hard. The sinkerball is perhaps the most difficult pitch to identify. In order to know whether to

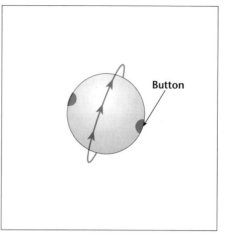

**FIGURE 12**
*A. The flight of a sinker.*

*B. The spin and button on a sinker.*

be alert for the pitch, the batter must watch the pitcher's warmup. Since identifying the sinker in flight is almost impossible, the hitter must depend more on the odds of the pitch being thrown.

Suppose the pitcher has a good hard sinker. The hitter can only hope he doesn't have a good slider as well. Such a pitcher can then do what hitters call "splitting the plate," that is, the pitcher has one pitch that goes in toward the batter and another that goes away from the batter. This makes him the toughest pitcher to hit. Each pitch starts out like a fastball, but the sinker drops down and in and the slid-

er moves away horizontally. A hitter will frequently have the same problem with a left-handed pitcher. A left-hander's fastball naturally sinks or runs away most of the time. His breaking ball comes down and in on the hitter, making it seem as though he's "splitting or peeling" the plate—one pitch goes one way and the other goes the opposite way.

To hit a sinker, the player must move away a few inches from the plate—not back toward the catcher, but perpendicular to the plate. He should also move up a few inches in the box toward the pitcher. This gives him a better chance of hitting the ball before it gets to its maximum sinking point. If the hitter is too deep in the box, he will find it hard to hit anything but the top of the ball, which results in a ground ball. The hitter may also try to use a slight inside-out swing in order to hit the inside portion of the ball. Most of the time the player will be hitting toward right centerfield. If possible, he should try to get the pitcher to throw the ball up in the zone. Although the pitch will run in to the batter, it will not sink as it will when it's down. Most opposite-field hitters tend to hit sinkers well because they swing inside out on the ball.

To gauge how effective a sinkerball pitcher will be on a given day, it helps to know how tired he may be. Most sinkerball pitchers are more effective when they are tired because they lose some velocity, which helps the ball sink. Studying game statistics in newspapers might help determine a pitcher's fatigue.

*Changeup.* A **changeup** is another pitch designed to look like a fastball, but it is held differently by the pitcher so that its speed is much slower. If the hitter recognizes it, he can adjust his timing accordingly. This can be done by raising the hands slightly, sitting with the legs, or by some cocking that delays the swing and allows the ball to get into the hitting area at the appropriate time.

*Forkball /*
*Split-Finger Fastball.*
Figure 13(a) shows the flight of a **forkball** or a **split-finger fastball**. Each pitch makes a sudden drop at the end, but the split-finger is faster. The ball is held by spreading, or "splitting," the fingers onto the sides of the ball. This grip slows the ball, causing the sudden drop at the end of the pitch (see Figure 13b).

To hit a forkball or a split-finger fastball, the hitter should position himself with a wider stance, thus lowering his vision by 4 to 6 inches. If the ball then drops, it will look from the lower position as though it is dropping only 3 to 4 inches. From a normal stance, the pitch looks as though it will drop a foot. Getting his eye level closer to that of the pitch gives the hitter a longer view and therefore the best possible vision in seeing that pitch.

One word of warning must be given on using the wider stance. This position makes the hitter more susceptible to the inside fastball. This is to his ad-

**FIGURE 13**
*A. The flight of a forkball or split-finger fastball.*

*B. The grip on a split-finger fastball.*

vantage, however, if he uses it to set up the pitcher, making him think he's looking for that forkball when he's actually looking for a fastball.

One always hopes that a pitcher does not have a good low fastball to go along with the forkball or split-finger fastball. Such a pitcher generally throws the fastball low and then uses the split-finger or forkball low and in the same area to make the pitches look the same. One comes in straight for a strike and then the next drops off. Thus the hitter must try to make the pitcher get the ball up in the zone and stay off any low pitches. The strategy is similar to that used with a good

high fastball pitcher. The hitter wants to make him concentrate on getting the ball down in the zone, because the pitch down appears basically straight. Although in fact no pitch can rise, it appears to do so if the ball is up in the zone.

*Knuckleball.* A **knuckleball** is a pitch that does not spin, but tends to float to the plate. Thus of all pitches, it is the most affected by the movement of the air and wind that happen to pass over it. That wind may catch a stitch and cause the ball to break in one direction, but then catch another stitch and break in another direction. Neither the pitcher nor the catcher can predict the flight of a knuckleball. The catcher even uses an oversized mitt to catch this pitch. So, how can a hitter know where the pitch is going? There is no foolproof method for hitting the knuckleball. About all the hitter can do to combat a knuckleball is keep in mind that the pitch is slower, so he has to wait on it. He can also move up in the box in order to get to the ball sooner before some other unexpected break occurs. Then he can try to hit a pitch up in the strike zone, waiting until the last possible moment to swing.

In truth, there are no foolproof secrets or tips to hitting any kind of breaking pitch. The hitter can only try to raise his probability of success by constantly adapting. Suppose that a pitcher is not throwing sinkers, but is throwing high fastballs. In this case, the batter would be ill-advised to position himself down in a wide stance—he could never get to those pitches. He would need to straighten up a bit, narrow his stance, and get deeper in the box in order to give himself the maximum time to get to the ball. The hitter should always keep in mind that moving around in the batter's box serves a purpose.

# 9. Setting Up the Pitcher

Sometimes a hitter can set up the pitcher to throw what he wants. For example, suppose the pitcher has thrown the batter seven curveballs and has gotten him out every trip to the plate. In this case, on his next at bat, the batter can try to set up the pitcher by the way he stands in the box. He gets right on top of the plate to make the pitcher think that he's looking for the curveball again when he is actually expecting an inside fastball. Seeing the batter on top of the plate, the pitcher and the catcher then think that they can get him out on an inside fastball. Most of the time the catcher makes this determination by looking at the batter's feet. They play right into the batter's hands. The batter wants no part of the curveball and prepares to pounce on the inside fastball. In order to hit the inside fastball from this awkward position close to the plate, the hitter has to make sure to use his hips and hands, bringing his hands down across his body into the hitting zone.

There are many different ways in which to set up the pitcher. Suppose a

**FIGURE 14**
*Foot adjustments.*

pitcher is throwing all inside fastballs and the batter is not getting around to hit them. He can set up the pitcher by backing off the plate and making him think he's looking for more inside fastballs. In reality, he might be expecting a pitch on the outside part of the plate. By backing off the plate, the batter sets up the pitcher to stop throwing inside and start throwing outside.

This tactic works best when the hitter knows his own abilities and feels confident that he can hit a pitch that the pitcher thinks will get past him. In truth, the hitter has nothing to lose, because he is not hitting the other kind of pitch, say, the curve. If the pitcher does persist in throwing that curve, however, the hitter is in a better position to hit it.

These are just some of the little games that a hitter can play with a pitcher. Suppose the hitter is swinging way ahead of the pitch. One trick is to rotate his back foot slightly at an angle (see Figure 14a), which makes his turning radius larger. Another tactic, if a pitcher is throwing exceptionally hard, is to narrow the position of his feet, cutting down the turn and radius of his back foot (see Figure 14b).

*A. To avoid swinging way ahead of the pitch, rotate the toe of the back foot toward the catcher.*

*B. For an exceptionally hard-throwing pitcher, narrow the position of the feet to cut down the turn.*

## 10. Gardening at the Plate

Often you will see a batter doing "gardening work," that is, smoothing out the dirt in the batter's box. This may seem like nothing more than a nervous habit or a desire to eliminate the holes left by the preceding batter. There is more to this than meets the eye, however, for the advanced hitter. The hitter is actually checking his stride. He can see where he started and where he landed, and the stride can actually tell him if he landed too hard.

In between pitches, the hitter is checking to see if he is carrying out certain parts of his swing and stride. Is he stepping in a bucket or locking himself too close to the plate? If the area is cleaned off properly, his feet aren't going to lie to him. Some hitters are convinced that they are not stepping on home plate when they are. Then they wonder why they're not getting around on the ball. Others step away from the ball and cannot reach the outside part of the plate. Smoothing out the dirt in the box gives the hitter clear evidence of what he's doing and what he's not doing.

The information that this gardening provides the more advanced hitter allows him to make immediate corrections between pitches and possibly correct a poor night. Although all hitters make changes sometimes from game to game, the player at the higher level makes adjustments from one at bat to the next, and sometimes even from one pitch to the next.

## 11. Fungos, Pepper, and Music

A *fungo* is a light bat with a thin diameter. If a player is struggling at the plate, it can be quite beneficial for him to hit balls to infielders with a fungo bat. Fungo hitting also helps a player who is having trouble seeing the ball, pulling his head, or uppercutting. He can work himself back into the habit of watching the ball and imagining the ball coming off the bat. Then he can begin to tell what he is doing when swinging. If he is swinging inside out too often, he will cut the ball outside. If he is swinging up, he will hit pop-up line drives to the infielders when he is actually trying to hit ground balls. A lot of professionals will ask their coach if they should hit fungos when they're not feeling right about their hitting.

Hitting one-handed pepper to isolate their hands is also beneficial for advanced hitters. This allows them to determine which hand is dominant. Such knowledge can be valuable when a player injures one hand and must compensate by making greater use of the other hand.

"When a player is not hitting well, it is often because he doesn't have any rhythm, is not seeing the ball well, or has a quick front side."

When a player is not hitting well, it is often because he doesn't have any rhythm, is not seeing the ball well, or has a quick front side. If he is hitting well, he just relaxes. Many advanced hitters like to listen to music to help them relax and to get some rhythm in their hitting. This music can be provided by a public address system or by a portable stereo. Some players like rhythm and blues, some jazz, rock and roll, or country/western. Dusty Baker used rhythm and blues or jazz, because he felt that it got him into a flow like dancing.

## 12. Hitting Clues from the Defense

The advanced hitter should be alert to the many clues given by the pitcher and the catcher as to what pitch will be thrown. For example, sometimes a noisy catcher has old shinguards. If the hitter hears the shinguards rattle around behind him, it probably indicates that the catcher is moving to the inside or outside to set up the hitter for a certain pitch. The hitter might choose to take a pitch to see if he is right. If he is, he can then react accordingly.

Sometimes the more advanced hitters can watch the second baseman, shortstop, or centerfielder for clues as to how the pitcher will be throwing the ball. Suppose the opposition has decided to pitch inside to the hitter and plays the defense to pull. Then the third baseman will be on the line, the shortstop will be closer to third base (in the hole), and the centerfielder will be over toward left center. This alerts the hitter to two possibilities: The pitcher is going to throw either fastballs or something off speed. The game situation or the score might also be clues, but at least the hitter has a better idea of what to expect.

Other clues can come from a player's past history with a particular pitcher. Suppose that for the past three years he has been getting breaking balls from a pitcher. Clearly, the hitter should look for a breaking ball or something off speed. As we have said, it is best for a hitter to look for a fastball and adjust. Sometimes, however, if the pitcher gets into a pattern, the batter must give in, change his expectations, and sit on certain pitches.

Occasionally a shortstop moves just before the pitcher winds up. If he moves toward the second-base bag, he is probably expecting the pitch to be something hard and away because the opposition expects the hitter to hit that ball up the middle. As another example, suppose that the second baseman, centerfielder, and rightfielder shade the batter to right field. Then because the defense is playing the batter away, the hitter might expect the pitch to be away.

Often smart defenders use moves to deceive the batter. They show the hitter one defense and then move back just before the pitcher winds up.

The more advanced hitter must also be able to recognize who's in charge.

Suppose there is a veteran catcher behind the plate and a rookie pitcher on the mound. Remember, a pitcher's best friend is the catcher. In such a situation, it will most often be the catcher, and not the rookie pitcher, who will decide what and how a pitch will be delivered.

On the other hand, suppose there is a veteran pitcher on the mound and a rookie catcher behind the plate. Then the hitter should, by and large, forget the catcher. If both the pitcher and the catcher are veterans, then the hitter is in a tough position.

The advanced hitter must learn the catcher's patterns. Sometimes certain catchers (and teams) fall into patterns. For instance, if the hitter takes a good cut at a pitch and fouls it straight back, then on the next pitch, the catcher may always call for a changeup.

The hitter also has to consider the catcher in other ways. Suppose there is a superb catcher with a great arm who doesn't like anybody running on him. Let's assume as well that there is a fast runner on first base. This type of catcher will often call for fastballs away in this case so that he can more easily throw the runner out at second base. If the runner at first base is not fast, then the catcher might call for any kind of pitch because the defense is not worried about the runner stealing.

Some catchers even like to call for a breaking ball with a man on third base so that they can block the pitches in the dirt and show off their defensive skills. Still others with a man on third base will not call any pitches that are tough to catch, such as a split-finger or a hard-slider. They will call only for a fastball or a changeup because they don't want any passed balls or wild pitches allowing that run to score from third base. Thus many factors go into the overall equation that determines the effect of the catcher, all of which fall into the category of guessing, or artful anticipation, on the part of the advanced hitter.

The hitter can also find many clues to pitches in the pitcher's habits. Nearly every pitcher does something a little bit different with his breaking ball. What the hitter should watch from the dugout or from the on-deck circle is the pitcher's windup. To get more power on the fastball, a pitcher will come up higher over his head than he does with the breaking ball. His windup will not be nearly as high on the breaking ball because he is trying to slow his body down so the ball will break. One pitcher currently in the National League comes over his head on a fastball and to the side on a slider. The difference is ever so slight, but the alert hitter can pick up and make good use of such clues.

A relief pitcher often has his adrenaline pumping because he enters the game in a pressure situation. Let's say he throws a sinker but has a nervous habit of putting the ball behind his back and twirling it in his hand. This is visible to the hitter. The pitcher takes the sign, not changing his grip, and abruptly stops, giving an instant clue to the hitter. The hitter then sits on the sinker and gets a hit. More recently, many pitchers are holding the forkball in a special way behind the back. The clever pitcher, however, might just try to trick the hitter with such a clue. The hitter may think he has him outsmarted, but does not. *The game within a game continues*! The hitter has to know who is tricking him and who is not.

Some pitchers charge the hitter with their fastball but throw the breaking ball tentatively by slowly stepping toward the plate. Still others have their hands way up to throw a split-finger fastball or changeup. The hitter may see the pitcher's wrists as he takes the ball over his head in the windup. But on a breaking ball, the hitter might not see as much of the pitcher's wrist. Although these differences are ever so slight, any that the hitter can pick up will only contribute to his success at the plate.

Quite often a player will get upset in batting practice when the pitcher doesn't tell him what kind of pitch will be thrown. Although there are some players who do not want to know the pitch, most look for any kind of tip to help identify the pitch more quickly, especially in a game. As we mentioned earlier, the hitter should watch a pitcher warm up. Suppose the pitcher throws five curveballs and can't get any of them over the plate. Then the hitter might scratch that pitch from the pitcher's repertoire for that day. Now instead of having three effective pitches that game, the pitcher has only two. If he throws the batter a fastball for a strike, he might have to throw it again because his curveball is not working and he doesn't want to throw a changeup.

This clue raises the odds of the hitter's success.

As another example, let's assume that during his warmup all of a particular pitcher's fastballs are high. The hitter should then look for the fastball down and not necessarily even swing at the fastball high, letting such pitches go as balls. Another clue can be picked up by watching the pitcher when he comes into the game and is warming up on the mound. If he begs for two more pitches, then the hitter knows he is not feeling positive about his ability. On the other hand, if the pitcher comes in and takes only four of his eight given warmup pitches, he is probably fairly confident.

The hitter should also think about who is in the on-deck circle. Would the pitcher rather face him or the man on deck? If he would rather face the hitter at the plate because the next batter hits him well, it may be humbling but the hitter has to accept it. The pitcher might then throw the batter tough pitches, trying to get him to fish for something that he doesn't want to hit. These games within a game may seem very complicated, but they are a reality that the advanced hitter must face.

**FIGURE 15**
*Hitting an inside pitch to the opposite field.*

*A. Method 1: Stand on top of the plate, bail out, and drag the hands through the zone.*

*B. Method 2: Stand away from the plate and stride into the ball, creating an angle. Drop the back foot in order to close the stance.*

## 13. Hitting to the Opposite Field

Good hitters can hit *any* kind of pitch —whether inside, middle, and outside—to the opposite field. The best opposite-field hitters prefer taking an inside pitch to the opposite field to taking a ball outside. There are two ways to hit an inside pitch to the opposite field:

1.  The hitter stands on top of the plate, bails out, and drags his hands through the zone (see Figure 15a).

2.  The hitter stands away from the plate at the outset and then strides into the ball, creating an angle. But the further the hitter is from the plate, the more he has to drop his back foot in order to close his stance. This keeps the angle the same going to the opposite field (see Figure 15b). Most pitchers tend to throw inside to an opposite-field hitter. The hitter just fights this off by using the proper bat angle.

Most opposite-field hitters do not like off-speed or breaking pitches because it is hard to wait for those pitches and then hit them to the opposite field. Ironically, most pitchers throw hard to opposite-field hitters. These hard pitches also tend to be inside, which is actually just what such hitters prefer. Since the defense is playing the batter most often to the opposite field, the pitcher does not like to throw off-speed or breaking pitches. The slower pitches tend to speed up the hitter's bat, because he has a hard time waiting for the pitch, and make him pull the ball away from the defense. The defense is shifted over—everybody knows the ball is going to be hit to the opposite field. If the pitcher throws a slow pitch, however, the batter pulls the ball and gets it into a big hole in the defense. Thus a good opposite-field hitter has a real edge. First of all, he knows he can handle an inside fast-ball, and second, he has a defensive advantage in case a slow pitch is thrown.

To hit an outside pitch to the opposite field, it helps to allow some bend in the front leg. Although the goal is always to hit off a firm front side, it is difficult to hit an outside pitch effectively with a good bat angle off a stiff front leg (see Figure 16). The bending movement in the front leg is similar to

**FIGURE 16**
*Hitting an outside pitch to the opposite field: Allow some bend in the front leg similar to a leg thrust.*

a leg thrust, while the back foot stays in the same position that it does with any other swing.

The game within a game goes on as follows. Let's say that the player is an opposite-field hitter. He wants a hard inside pitch and the pitcher will generally throw it to him. A crafty pitcher, however, might give him an off-speed pitch or inside curve. The hitter will then pull it foul on purpose, letting the pitcher think he cannot take that pitch to the opposite field. Does the pitcher throw another inside pitch? Has the pitcher misled the hitter or has the hitter misled the pitcher? Now the game is really going on between the batter and the pitcher. The hitter must decide which pitches are for a particular purpose and which are not. Most pitchers come inside with one pitch for a reason, but if they come inside twice in a row, the hitter's mind could bounce between that inside pitch and some other, creating doubt about the patterns of the pitcher.

## 14. Knowing the Opposition's Philosophy

The first thing a major league hitter wants to know is who the opposition's pitching coach is. Knowing the basic philosophies of the pitching coach or instructor in the opposing organization gives the hitter a fairly good idea of how he might be pitched. Certain organizations like to pitch fastballs up and in. Suppose the opposition keeps the ball away from the hitter until there are two strikes, and then comes inside. They might also tend to pitch like their pitching coach or, if the team has the talent, it might choose

the pattern of pitches that its stars use. For example, the Los Angeles Dodgers might choose to pitch like Don Sutton, and at one time all of the Chicago Cubs were pitching like Ferguson Jenkins. Thus it helps if the hitter learns to think along with the opposition's pitching coach.

The hitter also has to think about what the opposing team thinks *he* can do. If it thinks he is a high-ball hitter because he has hit many high balls in the past, then the hitter must watch for pitches in other locations. If the opponent's pitching philosophy is simply to pitch down, then he must watch for low pitches. If the player has hit this team's pitcher well in the past, then he must assume that the opposition will make some adjustments to stop him from hitting that well the next time. Also, most teams will pitch the hitter differently with the bases empty than with men on base. The hitter has to realize this difference. The game of baseball is one of constant adjustment and readjustment. Clearly, the hitter goes to the plate with his brain as well as his bat!

All of this thinking supports what was discussed earlier about getting deep in the count on the first at bat. Doing so allows the hitter to make a determination of how the opposition is trying to pitch him that game.

## 15. Knowing the Umpires

Knowing the umpire behind the plate is another important factor in the advanced hitter's success. Some umpires tend to be pitchers' umpires, calling close pitches strikes more often than not, while others are batters' umpires, calling the same close pitches balls more often than not. Some umpires are high-ball umpires; that is, they tend to call high-pitch strikes. Others are low-ball umpires, and for those the hitter must be sure to swing if he has two strikes on him. Still other umpires have a loose strike zone early in the game to keep the game rolling but tighten up the strike zone later.

The stature of an umpire will be a factor in his calls. For example, a tall umpire may tend to call high pitches strikes because he can see them well. But he may call low pitches balls because he cannot get down to them as well. On the other hand, a short umpire might tend to call low pitches strikes because he can see them well and call high pitches balls because they look high to him.

Knowing the umpire is important at the college level as well, where hitters see the same umpires many times over. An unknowing hitter may return from the plate complaining of a bad call on a low pitch when actually the umpire had been making those same calls during the entire game and possibly many games before. Watching from the bench might have made that hitter better prepared.

## 16. Varying Bat Sizes and Stances

At the advanced level, hitters are gravitating to lighter and lighter bats. Actually many could benefit by using a little heavier bat, letting that extra weight supply the energy to the ball rather than trying to achieve everything with bat speed. Bat weight is still a factor in hitting.

The advanced hitter can do some subtle experimenting with different stances in order to combat various pitchers or various pitches being thrown by the opposition. If he is being thrown a lot of breaking balls, he might try to sit back on his back foot to see the ball better. At the same time, he should move up in the box a bit in order to see the ball all the way. If the opposition is throwing mostly fastballs, he should move out of a crouch, if he has one, and consider standing straighter at the plate. He may also want to move back slightly in the box.

# 17. The Hitter's Triangle

Every hitter has a rectangle formed by the strike zone within which he hits. Almost all hitters also have a *triangle* inside the rectangle within which they prefer to hit the ball (Figure 17).

Most right-handed batters first like the ball up and away, which is indicated in Figure 17(a) by (1). Second, they like the ball low and in, which is illustrated in Figure 17(a) by (2). Third, they like the ball up and in. Most right-handers do not like and have trouble with the pitch that is low and away.

Most left-handed batters have different preferences (see Figure 17b). First, they like the ball low and in. Second, they like the ball up and away. Third, they like the ball low and away. They do not like and have trouble with the pitch that is up and in.

As you can see, both the triangles and the order of preference differ. Such a

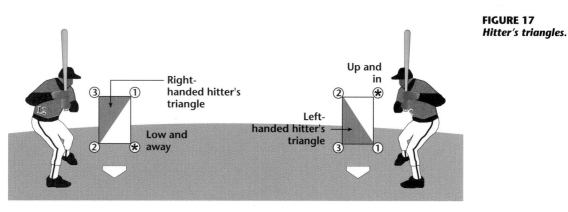

**FIGURE 17**
*Hitter's triangles.*

**A. Right-handed hitter.**     **B. Left-handed hitter.**

difference might be because hitters typically face right-handed pitching more often than left-handed pitching.

This information helps a pitcher as well as the hitter. For example, knowing those triangles might keep the pitcher from throwing a down and in pitch to a left-handed batter. The pitcher might also keep the ball low and away to a right-handed batter.

**"A right-hander who is a low-ball hitter has a definite advantage, because pitchers are being taught to keep the ball down to them. Pitchers are also being taught to keep the ball up to left-handed batters, since they tend to be low-ball hitters. In general, the best hitters are high-ball left-handers and low-ball right-handers."**

Consequently, the pitches seen most often at the professional level are split-finger fastballs, forkballs, sinkers, and breaking balls. This has forced many right-handed hitters to become low-ball hitters. A right-hander who is a low-ball hitter has a definite advantage, because pitchers are being taught to keep the ball down to them. Pitchers are also being taught to keep the ball up to left-handed batters, since they tend to be low-ball hitters. In general, the best hitters are high-ball left-handers and low-ball right-handers.

## 18. Spring Training

The advanced hitter should arrive at spring training or the beginning of practice in good physical condition. Most important is that he keep his weight down. Next he should be sure to work on his legs and arms because they take the longest to get in good shape. At the very least, the player should have been running frequently and doing some weight training routinely.

During spring training, it may help the player to pace himself, especially if he has the luxury because of his status on the team. Ideally the player wants to peak for the beginning of the season but not too early in spring training, because it is difficult to maintain peak performance for a long period of time. The player strives for a certain balance. He wants to be ready, but not burned out. On the other hand, if the player is trying to *make* the team, he usually has no choice but to go all out during spring training.

Once the player has established his place on the team, his main task is to get in tiptop shape, perfecting his hand–eye coordination as well as toughening his hands and feet as soon as possible. He wants his feet tough so he doesn't get sore and blistered. He wants to get those aches and pains out of the body as soon as possible.

Spring training is the place for the player to judge whether he is ready or not, rather than a place to measure how many hits he is getting. Everyone would prefer to get hits. But often a major league hitter will have one of his best years when he was in top shape in spring training, but didn't really hit that well at that time.

If a player leaves spring training injured, his entire season becomes an uphill struggle. Because baseball is played virtually every day, a player just does not have time to heal. If he is injured on Monday, he will probably

**Marv.** *Just how has the emergence of the relief pitcher affected the game?*

**Dusty**. Very few pitchers are going the distance anymore. With the emergence of long-, middle-, and short-relief specialists, the hitter has a good chance of facing, at a minimum, two or three quality pitchers in the course of a game. Therefore, it's hard for the hitter to set up a pitcher for that third or fourth at bat because the original pitcher will probably not be around. So the professional coach has to recognize what the opposition is doing to his hitters as well as teach the fundamentals.

**Marv.** *How do you deal with the effects of hitting coaches who have preceded you?*

**Dusty**. Generally, you try not to totally disagree with his primary past instructor, whether it's a college, high school, or other coach, or the player's dad. You have to listen to the other coach's theories and philosophies before enacting your own. It's always possible that they are similar, but just expressed in a different way.

still be hurting on Tuesday or Wednesday. So the main goal of spring training is to leave healthy, in a good frame of mind and ready for the season. The season is not one month, but six. It's rather like a marathon— the player wants to run the entire race at a consistent pace if possible.

Part of a player's decision on how to approach spring training will be based on whether he is trying to make the team or trying to get ready. After a while he will know whether he is to be a starter or not. If he is, then his main task is to get ready for the season and keep from being injured. Thus he might take two at bats early in the spring and play three innings. Later, he might take three at bats and play five innings. Then he might play seven innings for three or four games. Finally, during the last ten days, he might try to go the full nine innings for the sake of endurance, if nothing else.

The worst thing a player can do is not get in baseball shape. A player can be in some kind of physical shape, yet not be in baseball shape. A player is in baseball shape if he is prepared for an extra-inning game early in the season and is physically geared for the entire season.

A typical spring training day for a major league hitting coach like Dusty Baker begins around 8:00 A.M. The team first takes bunting practice. Then it works on hitting fundamentals, followed by batting practice and infield practice. Next the players do some outfield and infield work, and the pitchers work on covering first base. After the first ten days or so, the team begins its exhibition games. After some games, there is extra batting practice for players who feel they need the work. At this point, it is important to treat all players the same. Since the team does not know who will be important as the season progresses, slighting the rookies who are trying to make the club would be a poor tactic.

## 19. Bat Vibrations and Sweet Spots*

Have you ever heard a player saying "I hit the sweet spot" or "I hit the ball so well I barely felt it"? Considering the physics of a baseball bat as it hits a ball helps us understand what this means. First of all, when a bat is swung at a ball, it is a firm *rotating* object. It makes sense then that the speed and quickness of that rotation has an effect on the ball.

But after the bat hits the ball, it becomes a *vibrating* object. Though this vibration is not visible to the naked eye, the batter definitely feels it to one degree or another. To understand how the vibration takes place, take a piece

*We wish to thank Robert K. Adair of Yale University and Mark Reuber of Grove City College for their kind and helpful conversations regarding this topic.

YOU CAN TEACH HITTING

of metal sheeting about 2 inches wide and 5 feet long. Hold it in the middle and shake it. The result resembles a vibrating bat (see Figure 18). Note that vibrations can be seen in the middle, where it is being shaken, and on the ends, but there are two locations where there seem to be no vibrations. These locations are called *nodes*, and locations of greatest vibration are called *antinodes*.

Though they are not visible, vibrations occur when the bat hits the ball. There are two nodes on a bat, one in the handle and one up in the barrel. Hopefully, the ball does not hit the handle node because that is where the bat is held. But the ball can hit the barrel node. That node is called the **sweet spot** (see Figure 19).

If the ball hits near a node, there is very little, if any, vibration. If the ball hits an antinode, there is maximum vibration, possibly as much as one half inch. This explains why the greatest stinging effect occurs if a ball is hit on the antinode just above the handle. If it hits anywhere other than on a node, a vibration is created. Any vibration, no matter how slight, takes energy away from the ball, shortening the distance that it travels off the bat.

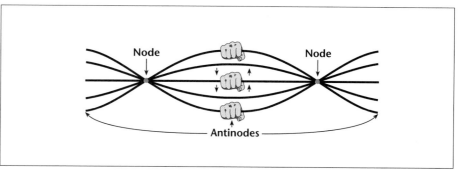

**FIGURE 18**
*The nodes and antinodes of a vibrating strip of metal.*

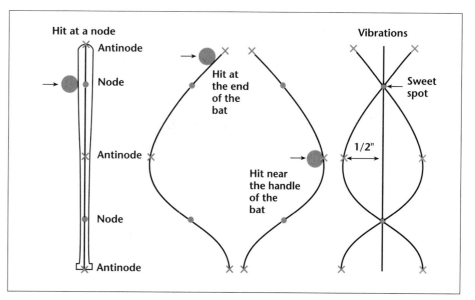

**FIGURE 19**
*The nodes, antinodes, and sweet spot of a vibrating bat. (Reprinted with permission from **The Physics of Baseball** by Robert K. Adair, New York: Harper Collins Publishers, 1990, p. 91).*

> We wish you many hits on the "sweet spot"!

You can actually "hear" where the nodes are on a wooden bat by screwing a hook into the top end of the bat and hanging it vertically from the ceiling. Put some adhesive tape on the end of a hammer and move from one end of the bat to the other, tapping the bat with the hammer. The changes in sound will indicate the position of the nodes and places in between. The hitter could place a piece of tape on the sweet spot. The node or sweet spot on a metal bat is longer than on a wooden bat, but it cannot be discovered in the manner we just described because of the air shaft inside the bat. The longer sweet spot on a metal bat is another hitting advantage of metal over wooden bats.

Brian Spurlock

YOU CAN TEACH HITTING

## Conclusion

In conclusion, our advice to the young hitter is to keep in mind that for most of those who have played professional baseball, that goal started out as just a dream. You will never really know how close the dream is until you just continue to try, work hard, and do your best. Those dreams can be fulfilled, just like those in other aspects of your life, if you stay with them and are dedicated. With luck, you have enough God-given athletic ability to even try. But if not, remember that there are a million different ways to be successful in life.

For more help, see the following Appendix.

Good luck and great hits!

Dusty, Jeff, and Marv

# Appendix

## Where
## Do You Go From Here?

To help you beyond what we've discussed here, we have available a video series to supplement the book. You'll see a handy order form at the end of this appendix to make it easy to order your copy. If you want to order a copy of this book, you can also use a separate order form at the end of this appendix. We can also give you extra hitting instruction in two other ways: One is the *Dusty Baker School of Baseball* and the other is the *Jeff Mercer's Personal Hitting Instructor*.

## Dusty Baker School of Baseball

Each summer, usually in July and August, the *Dusty Baker School of Baseball* meets in Sacramento, California. Owned by Dusty Baker and Gene Frechette, the school has several sessions broken down into age groups: ages 8–11, 12–14, and a Special Advanced Session for Ages 15–19. It is a live-in professional baseball school with lodging at Sacramento State University and the Training Site at Rancho Cordova Park, in Sacramento County. This school, endorsed by the San Francisco Giants and the Oakland Athletics, includes instruction on all aspects of baseball with a special emphasis on hitting and pitching. Instructors include Dusty Baker as well as nine other major leaguers, minor leaguers, and major league scouts. Some of the major league instructors—including Jim Barr, Bob Oliver, Mike Sadek, Jim Willoughby, Billy North, and Curt Brown—have been with the school since its inception. The goal of the school is to bring the students back each year until they repeat a minimum of two years and have passed through the Special Advanced Session for Ages 15–19.

Besides the instruction, the school provides a custom baseball jersey and cap, trophies, awards, and a trip to see an Oakland Athletic or San Francisco Giant night baseball game. The sleeping dorms are supervised by counselors and instructors, but day students are also welcome.

The school is operated by Dusty Baker, president; Gene Frechette, vice president and Atlanta Braves scout; and Oscar Miller and Guy Anderson, field coordinators. For more information, write

*Dusty Baker School of Baseball*
*69420 Crooked Horseshoe Rd.*
*Sisters, Oregon 97759*

The following are excerpts from a newspaper article, recently printed by a local newspaper. It is reprinted with permission of Neighbors-NE.

# The King Holds Court

## by
## Pete LeBlanc

Photo courtesy *Neighbors Magazine*, by Randy Allen

Through the eyes of a 10-year-old, this was baseball paradise. Ex-big leaguers wearing sparkling white uniforms—real ones—were everywhere. And they were serving up enough lectures and demonstrations on curveballs, suicide bunts, sliding techniques and anything else remotely related to baseball in an attempt to quench the appetite of all the fanatical big league wanna-bes.

It went on like that for five straight days, morning until night. But the grand slam of it all was when the king came to greet the inhabitants of his baseball paradise. To them, no moment was more exciting. That king would be Dusty Baker—ex-major leaguer and current batting coach of the Giants.

The 142 inhabitants were youngsters ranging in age from 8 to 12 years old. "Oh, jeez," said Gene Frechette, the vice-king who owns and operates 50 percent of the baseball school with Baker. "When they first see him walk through that gate, everyone yells, 'Dusty!' When he was still playing and he'd come up to bat, all the kids at the game would

be yelling. Oh, yeah! You bet your life. They love it."

"It's neat," said 10-year-old Dusty Kimura, a second-year camper who plays Little League. "Everyone tells him to come over and he'll go to all the different groups and sign autographs and stuff."

It would be easy to see how the king could just toss this aside as no big deal. After all,

Baker does more important matters to tend to such as assisting San Francisco's hitters. But for the king and the common folk, it is give and take in this village.

"They don't know it, but it's as equally exciting for me," Baker says. "This helps me improve my teaching skills. It helps me when I go back to the Giants. At the pro level, everything becomes so complicated and you can start overemphasizing theories and applications. Sometimes, you need to be here to get back to the basics, and I'll take that back to Will Clark, Kevin Mitchell or Matt Williams. Sometimes, I'll just look at a kid swing and that can help get you straightened out."

Frechette, a 61-year-old Rocklin, CA resident, former farmhand in the Washington Senators organization and present Braves scout, approached Baker in 1984 with the idea of the baseball camp. Dusty had just left the Dodgers as a free agent and was signed by the Giants. The rest is history. Frechette and Baker started with just over 100 students in 1985. This year, 375 students will attend.

Today, Baker still talks about a basketball camp he attended when he was a 16-year-old junior. Baker was the tournament most valuable player, his scoring average increased from 11 points to 20-plus by his senior year, and the self-esteem he gained at the camp is something Baker never forgot.

"I had wanted to start a camp when I was a rookie with the Braves," he said. "This was perfect. Like most things in life, they'll work out, just not on your schedule."

Though Frechette is not mentioned in the school's title, he handles most of the administrative duties. However, that is not to say that Baker is not involved with the camp. Though his schedule can make for a hectic day, Baker tries to make at least two appearances for each of the three one-week sessions when road games do not prevent him from doing so. Baker resents people who think he is involved with the camp in name only. "We're not like that," he said. "Gene does quite a bit of the duties and I keep as much hands on as I can and make sure things are being taught correctly."

"You feel like you could be somebody when you hear that Dusty Baker goofed off when he was a kid," said 12-year-old Craig Smalley, a first baseman. "I used to have an attitude like that, but now I know I have to listen to my coaches."

Baker and Frechette have plenty of help in getting students such as Smalley to think that way. Leading the charge is Field Coordinator Oscar Miller. A fast-talking motivator, the 48-year-old Miller handles most of the lectures at the camp, which include evening lessons and homework assignments.

Miller's job is to teach the students baseball, and he does it as if he is leading a high-impact aerobics class. All that's missing is the music. Miller barks out commands and the students respond quickly and accurately.

When Miller isn't lecturing or the students aren't eating, participating in a game, making their beds, doing their laundry or finishing a homework assignment, chances are they can be found at a station manned by a former major leaguer or minor leaguer. The students receive a minimum of four to five hours of instruction per day. Lectures at night reinforce the skills the players learned on the field during the day. And there are hustle pins, awards at the end of the camp, free posters and chances to win free equipment.

"It was tough at first," Baker said. "Three or four years ago, I didn't know. But we wanted to do it first-class. It's turned into a real nice thing. But I'm not surprised it's done well. When you surround yourself with quality people, you get quality results."

Spoken like a true king.

*Jeff Mercer's Personal Hitting Instructor*

# DO YOU WANT TO BE A BETTER HITTER?

- Hit for a better average
- Hit with more power
- Be able to analyze and correct your mistakes

## *Then You Could Use Your Own* PERSONAL HITTING INSTRUCTOR

Wouldn't it be nice to have your own Professional Hitting Instructor to assist you with your swing? **NOW YOU CAN!!** No matter where you live, no matter what time of year. Help is available at your convenience.

One of the nation's finest hitting instructors (specializing in ages 8–22) is going to personally evaluate your swing and provide you with suggestions and corrective measures, all in a simple, easy-to-follow program on your own VCR.

Jeff Mercer, owner of Mercer's Sport Center and co-author of "You Can Teach Hitting," has developed a program to help your hitter with his/her swing. While books and instructional videos are essential tools in the learning process—wouldn't it be great to watch yourself and your instructor working on your stroke?

It's as simple as this: send in the information coupon with your name and address, or give us a call, and we'll mail you a brochure detailing the entire program. If you wish to get started right away, call and we will explain the **Introductory Special** and the complete program.

---

Yes, I want more information about my own "PERSONAL HITTING INSTRUCTOR."

Additional information may be sent to

Name _____     Name _____

Address _____     Address _____

City_____ State____ Zip____     City_____ State____ Zip____

Age of Hitter Interested in the Program _____     Age of Hitter Interested in the Program _____

Send this coupon to:     **JEFF MERCER**
**MERCER'S SPORT CENTER**          **or call (317) 736-8453**
**R.R. 5, BOX 350H**
**FRANKLIN, IN 46131**

## You Can Teach
# HITTING

### Now Also Available Direct on Video!

**N**ow you can supplement the clear, easy-to-understand descriptions, action sequences and graphics you find in *You Can Teach Hitting* the book with the new three volume video set *You Can Teach Hitting.* This exciting new video series narrated by Dusty, Jeff and Marv includes:

### Volume 1.
**A Systematic Approach to Hitting (Approx. 60 min.)**

### Volume 2.
**The Ten Common Hitting Mistakes and How to Correct Them (Approx. 60 min.)**

### Volumes 3.
**Twenty Hitting Drills (Approx. 60 min.)**

**The excitement and color of live action enhanced with state of the art computer graphics!**

Shot entirely on high-grade, high-performance video-tape, *You Can Teach Hitting* combines on-camera hitting instruction - featuring Dusty Baker and Jeff Mercer–with action sequences, using colorful graphical computer-images. Together they take you from bat selection to a complete series of systematic drills.

**Sound hitting instruction that produces results!**

*You Can Teach Hitting* is not just another video of "celebrity" cameo hitting advice! Each volume in the series shares a single goal: to present a simple-to-follow, systematic approach to hitting that will help *everyone* get more out of their game.

*Buy all three videos and save $10.00 over single title prices.*

*Call with your order... Today!*
**1-800-228-1248**

# Give You Can Teach Hitting To Friends, Coaches, Or Your Favorite Hitter!

## It couldn't be easier!

By now, you know!... The book you're holding is absolutely required reading for the encouraging parent or the experienced coach who wants to teach hitting better. And for any hitter who wants to hit better.

And that's why we've made it easy for you to purchase additional copies for your friends who coach or friends who play the game.

**"Best buy! Buy all the videos... and get the book for half price."**

To order, simply complete the attached order form, specifying the number of additional copies you wish to order. Enclose a check or money order for the total amount of your order (include postage and handling) or specify the credit card to which you are charging your purchase.

*or call...*

## 1-800-228-1248

*and place your order today!*

# ORDER FORM

*Please rush my **You Can Teach Hitting** order by return mail to.*

Name _____    City _____    State _____

Street _____    Zip Code _____    Telephone No. _____

| Quantity | Item | Unit Price | Total Price |
|---|---|---|---|
| | **You Can Teach Hitting (Book)** | $24.95 | |
| | **You Can Teach Hitting (Video)** | | |
| | **Volume 1. A Systematic Approach to Hitting** | $19.95 | |
| | **Volume 2. The Ten Common Hitting Mistakes and how to Correct Them** | $19.95 | |
| | **Volume 3. Twenty Hitting Drills** | $19.95 | |
| | **You Can Teach Hitting (Complete video package)** | $49.95 | |
| | *Best Buy!* **You Can Teach Hitting (Complete video package plus the book)** | $62.95 | |

### Credit Card Ordering

☐ VISA
☐ MasterCard
☐ AMERICAN EXPRESS
☐ DISCOVER

_____
Cardholder name (Please Print)

_____
Signature

☐☐☐☐☐ ☐☐☐☐☐ ☐☐☐☐☐ ☐☐☐☐☐

☐☐☐☐☐                    ☐☐☐☐☐

Mastercard Interbank #          Card Expires:

| | |
|---|---|
| Additional | |
| Order Sub-Total | |
| Postage & Handling (10% of order sub-total) | |
| IN residents add 5% sales tax | |
| **Total enclosed** | |

**Bittinger Books P.O. Box 68618 Indianapolis, IN 46268**

# YOUR OWN PRINT

Would you like to have

your own frameable

14"x17" print of the

poem and illustration

"Alone at the Plate"?

Send a check or money order for $12.* to:
Bittinger Books
3011 Whispering Trail
Carmel, IN 46033
Or call: (317) 846-9136

* Includes S&H, Please allow 2 to 4 weeks for delivery

These gloves enhance the teaching and use of the *standard grip* as taught in the systematic approach to hitting in Chapter 2.

**GRIP-TEC**™
**BATTING GLOVE**
*by SARANAC*®

- 100% Deerskin
- "Tacky Leather" Strips Keep Bat Where it Belongs—in the Fingers!
- Gives that Line Drive Swing
- Won't Slip in the Hands
- Protects From Blisters and Calluses
- Flexible
- Durable—30 Day Guarantee!

# Index

Aaron, Hank, 57, 160, 186, 192
Adair, Robert K., 27, 219
Advanced hitter tips, 9, 20, 23, 25, 27, 33, 49, 57, 58, 89, 92, 110, 113, 116, 124
Allen, Dick, 26
Angling back foot out, 49
Antinodes, 219
Ashley, Steven, 27

Back foot lockout, 59–62
Bailing out, 50
Batting cage, 139
Baker, Dusty (Johnnie B.), 4, 9, 16, 48, 74, 106, 145, 160, 163, 164, 178, 187, 189, 217, 218
Balance, 17, 21–24
Balanced stance, 21
Bat angle, 17, 29
    mistake, 62
Bat selection, 17–19
Bat-behind-the-back-drill, 83–84, 143, 146, 151
Being natural, 189
Bittinger, Marv, 4, 7, 16, 48, 74, 106, 132, 160, 178, 187, 217
Boggs, Wade, 164, 191
Bostock, Lyman, 189
Bottom hand, 78
Box, 29
    improper, 30, 31, 54
    proper, 30, 31, 54
Box and bat angle, 17, 29–32
Box mistakes, 54

Brett, George, 191
Bunt
    offset method, 107–112
    pivoting around, 107
    sacrifice, 107–111
    squaring around, 107
    squeeze, 116
Bunt and run, 115–116
Bunt grip, 109
Bunt for a base hit, 112–114
Bunting station, 122
Bunt locations, 111
Butler, Brett, 193
Button, 196–198

Canseco, Jose, 31, 56, 57
Carew, Rod, 191
Center-field grip, 28
Cepeda, Orlando, 160
Chair drill, 64, 98–99
Changeup, 202
Charting pitches, 167
Choke grip, 26, 53
Clark, Will, 6, 24, 31
Closed stance, 24
Clues from the defense, 207–211
Corrections
    back foot lockout, 60–61
    box, 57
    dead stop hitter, 58
    fear of ball, 70
    follow-through, 68
    front shoulder early release, 66

grip, 52–54
head position, 70
quick hip, 66
stance, 50
stride, 51
tracking, 70
Counts and situations, 146
Counts-and-situations drill, 101
Curveball, 199–200

Dead stop hitter, 57–59
    correction for, 58
Depth at the plate, 17, 19–21
Distance at the plate, 17, 19–21
Driessen, Dan, 143
Drills, 74–103
    1-2-3, 51, 62, 66, 97, 142
    1-2-3-4, 59, 80, 142
    bat behind the back, 62, 83–84, 143, 146, 151
    chair, 64, 98–99
    counts and situations, 101, 146
    fence, 64, 66, 68, 75–76
    game time, 89–90, 142, 146
    high pitch, 91, 146
    hip thrust, 62, 99, 142
    iso bat, 99–101
    low pitch, 90–91
    mirror, 51, 54, 57, 59, 64, 66, 68, 92
    now, 66, 95–96
    one hand, 54, 68, 77–78
    overload, 65, 84–86
    right/left/middle, 78–80, 140, 141, 146

YOU CAN TEACH HITTING

Drills (*continued*)
    short screen, 51, 57, 59, 64, 68, 93–95, 154
    soft-toss breaker, 82
    spin hit, 51, 62, 64, 66, 68, 86–88
    up and down, 102
Doby, Larry, 185

Enhancing competition, 127–129
Enhancing concentration, 189
Erickson, Scott, 200

Fairly, Ron, 160
Fastball, 196–198
Fear of the ball, 70–71
Fence drill, 64, 66, 68, 75–76
Field
    middle, 78–79
    opposite, 78–79
    pull, 78–79
Firm front side, 181
Flyballs, 184
Focus the eyes, 17, 36
Follow-through, 17, 41–42, 66–68, 182
    correction, 68
    mistake, 66–67
    three eyes, 42
Forkball, 202–203
Franco, Julio, 54, 56
Front shoulder early release/quick hip, 65–66
    correction, 66
    mistake, 65
Fungos, 206

Game of ones, 187
Game-time drill, 89–90, 142, 146
Gardening at the plate, 206
Grip, 17, 25–29
    bunt, 109
    center-field, 28
    choke, 53
    corrections, 52–54
    left-field, 28
    modified, 26
    right-field, 28
    standard, 25, 52, 53
Grip mistakes, 52–54
Ground balls, 184
Guerrero, Pedro, 23
Gwynn, Tony, 191

Hammer position, 180
Handling failure, 168–173
Hand position mistakes, 69–70
Hershiser, Orel, 200
High-pitch drill, 91, 146
    tomahawk, 92
Hip-thrust drill, 62, 99, 142
Hit and run, 114–115
Hitch, 57
Hitter development, 132–157
    ages 4–7, 132–135
    ages 8–10, 135–140
    ages 11–12, 140–143
    ages 13–15, 143–149
    ages 16–18, 149–153
    ages 18 and older, 153–157
Hitter's triangle, 215–216
Hitting, definition of, 178
Hitting clues from defense, 207–211
Hitting flyballs, 184
Hitting groundballs, 184
Hitting special pitches, 195–204
    changeup, 202
    curveball, 199–200
    fastball, 196–198
    forkball, 202–203
    knuckleball, 203
    screwball, 200
    sinker, 200–202
    slider, 198–200
    slurve, 200
    split finger, 202–203
Hitting to opposite field, 211–213

Ike to Mike, 17, 40–41
Improper bat angle, 62
Improper box, 30, 31, 54
Inward turn, 17, 32–34, 58
Iso-bat drill, 99–101

Johnson, Davey, 160
Jones, Cleon, 160
Jorgenson, Spider, 4

Keep the head down, 40–41
Knuckleball, 203

Left-field grip, 28
Live hitting station, 122

Long-term dedication and goals, 174–175
Low-pitch drill, 90–91
L-screen, *see* Short screen

McCullough, Eli, 4
McDowell, Roger, 200
McGee, Willie, 23, 191
Mental game, 160–175
    handling failure, 168–173
    long-term dedication and goals, 174–175
    mental to practical: a typical trip to the plate, 173–174
    physical–mental preparation on game day, 161–163
    putting on a game face, 163–168
    thinking with pitchers, 165–168
Mental–physical combination, 185
Mental to practical: a typical trip to the plate, 173–174
Mercer, Jeff, 4, 106, 132, 163
Middle field, 78–79
Mirror drill, 51, 54, 57, 59, 64, 66, 68, 92
Mistakes in hitting, 48–72
    back foot lockout, 59
    bat angle, 62
    box, 54
    fear of the ball, 70–71
    grip, 52–54
    follow-through, 66–67
    hand position, 69
    stance/stride, 48–51
    stride, 50
    ten most common, 48–72
    tracking, 69
Modified grip, 26
Mota, Manny, 193
Motivation, 8
Mitchell, Kevin, 11, 57, 173
Murray, Eddie, 31
Music, 206

Nodes, 219
Non-at-bats, 188
Not wasting at-bats, 188
Now drill, 66, 95–96

1-2-3 drill, 51, 62, 66, 97, 142
1-2-3-4 drill, 59, 80, 142
Offensive weapons, 106–117

Offset method to bunt, 107–112
One hand, swinging with, 184
One-hand drill, 54, 68, 77–78
Open stance, 24
Opposite field, 78–79, 191
    hitting to, 79–80, 141
    outside pitch, 141
Opposition's philosophy, knowing,
    213–214
Overload drill, 66, 84–86

Parallel stance, 24
Peale, Norman Vincent, 160
Pena, Alejandro, 200
Pepper, 122, 206
Perez, Tony, 160
Philosophy, 5, 13
Physical–mental preparation
    before game day, 161–163
    on game day, 161–163
    putting on a game face, 163–168
Physics of baseball, 219–220
Pitchers
    setting up, 204–206
    thinking with, 165–168
Pitches, charting, 167
Pivoting around to bunt, 107
Positions in lineup, 150
Power hand, 78
Power hitting, 193–195
Power V, 179–181
Practice organization, 120–129
    enhancing competition, 127–129
    enhancing concentration, 189
    situational hitting, 125–127
    station work, 120–125
Proper box, 30, 31, 55
Putting on a game face, 163–168

Quick hip, 65–66

Rhodes, Dusty, 145
Right-field grip, 28
Right/left/middle drill, 78–80, 140, 141, 146
Rose, Pete, 192, 193
Ruth, Babe, 26

Sacrifice bunt, 107–111
Sandburg, Ryne, 31, 64
Screwball, 200
Setting up the pitcher, 204–206
Shapiro, Barry, 197
Short screen, 57
Short-screen drill, 51, 59, 64, 68, 93–95, 154
Sinker, 200–202
Situational hitting, 125–127
Slap the hands down, 38–39
Slider, 198–200
Slurve, 200
Smith, Reggie, 23, 54
Soft-toss breaker drill, 82
Spin and rotation, 196–198
Spin-hit drill, 51, 62, 64, 66, 68, 86–88
Split-finger fastball, 202–203
Splitting the plate, 201
Spot, sweet, 218–220
Spring training, 216–218
Squaring around to bunt, 107
Squeeze bunt, 116
Squishing the bug, 17, 36–38, 79
Stance/stride, mistakes, 48–51
Stance, 17, 21–24
    closed, 24
    corrections, 50
    open, 24
    parallel, 24
Standard grip, 25, 52, 53
Stargell, Willie, 160
Station work, 120–125
    bunt, 122
    live hitting, 122

pepper, 122, 206
    teework, 122
    whiffle-ball, 121
Step to swing, 181
Stepping into the bucket, 50
Stride, 17, 34–36
    corrections, 51
    mistakes, 50
Sweet spot, 218–220
Swing, 17, 36–45
    one-hand, 184
    tomahawk, 92
Systematic approach to hitting, 16–45

Tee work station, 122
Thompson, Robby, 134, 145
Three C's of hitting, 45
Three eyes, 42
Thrift, Syd, 197
Tomahawk swing, 92
Tracking, 69–70
Triangle, hitter's, 215–216
Two-strike hitting, 192–193

Umpires, knowing, 214
Up-and-down drill, 102

Varying bat sizes, 214, 215
Varying stances, 214, 215
Vibrations, bat, 218–220

Williams, Billy, 166
Williams, Matt, 24, 171
Williams, Ted, 193, 194
Weight transfer, 182
Whiffle balls, 134
Whiffle-ball station, 121
Wrist-roller device, 143

Yastrzemski, Carl, 54